CULTURES OF THE WORLD
China

mc Marshall Cavendish
Benchmark
New York

PICTURE CREDITS

Cover: © Steve Vidler/Superstock
Aldo Pavan/Lonely Planet Images: 3, 16 • Bill Wassman/Lonely Planet Images: 63 • Bradley Mayhew/Lonely Planet Images: 92, 122 • Brent Winebrenner/Lonely Planet Images: 87 • Bruce Dale/National Geographic/ Getty Images: 54 • ChinaFotoPress/Getty Images: 44, 48 • Christopher Herwig/Lonely Planet Images: 109 • Dallas Stribley/Lonely Planet Images: 98 • Felix Hug/Lonely Planet Images: 128 • Feng Li/Getty Images: 64 • Getty Images: 8, 56, 72, 76, 124, 130, 131 • Greg Elms/Lonely Planet Images: 66, 104 • Inmagine.com: 46, 95, 106, 108, 115, 116 • John Hay/Lonely Planet Images: 118 • Johnny Haglund/Lonely Planet Images: 12 • Keren Su/Lonely Planet Images: 1, 24, 32, 42, 60, 62, 71, 90 • Krzysztof Dydynski/Lonely Planet Images: 6, 7, 38, 68, 74, 80, 83, 102 • Lee Foster/Lonely Planet Images: 96 • Martin Moos/Lonely Planet Images: 15, 53 • Merten Snijders/Lonely Planet Images: 27 • Michael Coyne/Lonely Planet Images: 70, 88, 112, 106 • Neil Setchfield/ Lonely Planet Images: 5 • Phil Weymouth/Lonely Planet Images: 101 • Richard I'Anson/Lonely Planet Images: 19, 82, 86, 105, 114 • Stuart Dee /Lonely Planet Images: 58 • Tim Hughes/Lonely Planet Images: 73 • Tom Cockrem/Lonely Planet Images: 94 • Topical Press Agency/Getty Images: 33 • Universal History Archive/Getty Images: 36 • Wibowo Rusli/Lonely Planet Images: 51

PRECEDING PAGE
Miao children in traditional dress

Publisher (U.S.): Michelle Bisson
Writers: Peggy Ferroa, Elaine Chan, and Yong Jui Lin
Editors: Deborah Grahame-Smith, Stephanie Pee
Copyreader: Sherry Chiger
Designers: Nancy Sabato, Benson Tan
Cover picture researcher: Tracey Engel
Picture researcher: Joshua Ang

Marshall Cavendish Benchmark
99 White Plains Road
Tarrytown, NY 10591
Website: www.marshallcavendish.us

All Internet sites were correct and accurate at the time of printing. All monetary figures in this publication are in U.S. dollars.

Library of Congress Cataloging-in-Publication Data

Ferroa, Peggy Grace, 1959-
  China / Peggy Ferroa, Elaine Chan, and Yong Jui Lin. -- 3rd ed.
     p. cm. -- (Cultures of the world)
  Includes bibliographical references and index.
  ISBN 978-1-60870-991-5 (print) -- ISBN 978-1-60870-998-4 (ebook)
  1. China—Juvenile literature. I. Chan, Elaine. II. Yong, Jui Lin. III. Title.

DS706.F38 2013
951—dc23   2011042592

Printed in the United States of America
7 6 5 4 3 2 1

CONTENTS

CHINA TODAY

CHINA IS ONE OF THE MOST EXCITING, VIBRANT PLACES ON EARTH. In 1949, after a bloody civil war, China became the People's Republic of China (PRC) under communist rule led by Mao Zedong. In the years that followed, the country isolated itself from the outside world until Mao's death in 1976.

Economic reforms introduced in 1978 by Mao's successor, Deng Xiaoping, opened the door to foreign investors and put China back on the world stage. The reforms introduced free-market principles and spurred phenomenal economic growth that surprised even the reformers.

China today is a land of burgeoning opportunities. It is now the second-largest economy in the world, next to the United States, and has overtaken the United States as the world's largest manufacturer. China's economy has grown at a blistering 10 percent a year for the past 30 years, a rate that is necessary to absorb the 15 million new entrants into the job market (as much as the whole population of Cambodia or Ecuador) each year. It is evident to observers that China is poised to move from export dependency to developing its own internal market. Being the

Limestone pinnacles form a beautiful backdrop in Guangxi in northeast China.

largest creditor nation in the world, it owns approximately 20.8 percent of all foreign-owned U.S. Treasury securities.

Historically the cultural sphere of China has extended across East Asia as a whole, with Chinese religion, customs, and writing systems being adopted to varying degrees by neighbors such as Japan, Korea, and Vietnam. Throughout its history, China was the source of many major inventions. It also has one of the world's oldest written language systems. The first evidence of human presence in the region was found at the Zhoukoudian caves. It is one of the earliest known specimens of *Homo erectus*, now commonly known as the Peking Man, estimated to have lived from 300,000 to 780,000 years ago.

China is the most populous nation on earth, with the biggest workforce, and it is the third-largest country in the world by land area. It borders 15 other countries and has landscapes ranging from broad plains to expansive deserts to lofty mountain ranges, including vast areas of inhospitable terrain. The eastern half of the country, its seacoast fringed with offshore islands, is a region of fertile lowlands, foothills and mountains, deserts, steppes, and

Crowds of people in Stone Forest in Kunming.

subtropical areas. The western half of China is a region of sunken basins, rolling plateaus, and towering massifs, including a portion of the highest tableland on earth.

China's huge population is not good for its environment. It now has the dubious distinction of being the world's largest emitter of carbon dioxide, overtaking the United States. China is also the largest contributor to world levels of sulfur oxides, chlorofluorocarbons, and other ozone-depleting substances.

Although China's forest cover is only 20 percent, the country has some of the largest expanses of forested land in the world, making it a top target for forest-preservation efforts. In 2001 the United Nations Environment Programme (UNEP) listed China among the top 15 countries with the most "closed forest"—in other words, virgin old-growth forest or naturally regrown woods. A total of 12 percent of China's land area, or more than 274 million acres (111 million ha), is closed forest. However, UNEP also estimates that 36 percent of China's closed forests are facing pressure from high

Timber being unloaded at a sawmill.

population densities, making preservation efforts crucial. According to the Chinese government website, the central government invested more than ¥40 billion ($629 million) between 1998 and 2001 in protecting vegetation, farm subsidies, and conversion of farms to forests. Between 1999 and 2002, China converted 19 million acres (7.7 million ha) of farmland into forest.

Desertification remains a serious problem, consuming an area greater than that taken by farmlands. Although desertification has been curbed in some areas, it still is expanding at a rate of more than 26 square miles (67 square km) every year. A total of 90 percent of China's desertification occurs west of the imperial palaces of the Ming and Qing dynasties in Beijing and Shenyang.

Matching the pace of the burgeoning economy, some unethical entities always seek ways to earn money quickly by sacrificing principles and safety. There have been numerous incidents involving food safety in China, including the use of pesticides or other dangerous chemical additives as food preservatives or additives and the use of unhygienic starting materials as food ingredients.

The 2008 Chinese milk scandal, in which milk, infant formula, and other food materials were adulterated with melamine, received the most attention among food-safety incidents. By November 2008, China had reported an estimated 300,000 victims, with six infants dying from kidney stones and other kidney damage and another 860 babies hospitalized. Two people who were responsible for this atrocious disaster, Zhang Yujun and Geng Jinping, were sentenced to death. The former chairwoman of Sanlu Group, the company that distributed the melamine-contaminated milk powder, was sentenced to life in prison.

UNESCO SITES IN CHINA

FORBIDDEN CITY IN BEIJING With its landscaped gardens and many buildings (whose nearly 10,000 rooms contain furniture and works of art), the Forbidden City in Beijing constitutes a priceless testimony to Chinese civilization during the Ming and Qing dynasties. The seat of the country's supreme power for five centuries (1416—1911), it was declared a UNESCO World Heritage Site in 1987.

IMPERIAL PALACE IN SHENYANG The Imperial Palace of the Qing Dynasty in Shenyang consists of 114 buildings constructed between 1625 and 1783. It contains an important library and is a testament to the foundation of the last dynasty that ruled China, before it expanded its power to the center of the country. This palace then became auxiliary to the Imperial Palace in Beijing. This remarkable architectural edifice offers important testimony of the history of the Qing Dynasty in addition to the cultural traditions of the Manchu and other tribes in the north of China.

MAUSOLEUM OF THE FIRST EMPEROR The Terra-cotta Army is a collection of life-size terra-cotta sculptures depicting the armies of Qin Shi Huang, the first emperor of China. An example of funerary art, it was buried with the emperor in 210 B.C. to help guard his empire in the afterlife. The figures were discovered in 1974 by local farmers in Xi'an, Shaanxi Province.

The sculptures vary in height, according to their roles, with the tallest being the generals, and they include warriors, chariots, horses, officials, acrobats, strongmen, and musicians. It is estimated that in the three pits containing the Terra-cotta Army there were sculptures of more than 8,000 soldiers, 130 chariots with 520 horses, and 150 cavalry horses. The majority of the figures are still buried in the pits.

JIUZHAIGOU NATIONAL PARK Jiuzhaigou National Park is a nature reserve in the north of Sichuan, a province in southwestern China. It is known for its many multilevel waterfalls and colorful lakes and was declared a UNESCO World Heritage Site in 1992. It belongs to category V (Protected Landscape) in the International Union for Conservation of Nature (IUCN) system of protected-area categorization.

Jiuzhaigou's landscape is made up of high-altitude karsts shaped by glacial, hydrological, and tectonic activity. It lies on major fault lines on the diverging belt between the Qinghai-Tibet Plate and the Yangtze Plate. The rock strata are made up mostly of carbonate rocks such dolomite and tufa, as well as some sandstone and shale. The valley includes the catchment area of three gullies (which due to their large size are often called valleys themselves) and is one of the sources of the Jialing River, part of the Yangtze River system.

MOUNT EMEI SCENIC AREA The Mount Emei Scenic Area, including Leshan Giant Buddha Scenic Area, has been listed as a UNESCO World Heritage Site since 1996. The Leshan Giant Buddha was built during the Tang Dynasty (618—907). It is carved out of a cliff face that lies at the confluence of the Minjiang, Dadu, and Qingyi rivers in the southern part of Sichuan Province, near the city of Leshan. The stone sculpture faces Mount Emei, with the rivers flowing below its feet. It is the largest carved stone Buddha in the world, and at the time of its construction was the tallest statue in the world. It was not damaged by the 2008 Sichuan earthquake.

OLD TOWN OF LIJIANG The town has a history going back more than 800 years and was once a confluence for trade along the old Tea Horse Road. The Lijiang old town is famous for its orderly system of waterways and bridges. Recently the government started to develop additional "old city" sections adjacent to the site of the original old city. This is to accommodate the large number of tourists who walk the cobblestone streets (cars are not allowed in the old city), typically as part of package tours.

SICHUAN GIANT PANDA SANCTUARIES Located in southwest Sichuan Province, the Sichuan Giant Panda Sanctuaries are home to more than 30 percent of the world's highly endangered giant pandas. They are among the most important sites for the captive breeding of these animals. They cover 3,570 square miles (9,245 square km) with seven nature reserves and nine scenic parks in the Qionglai and Jiajin mountains. The sanctuaries are also a refuge for other endangered species, such as the red panda, the snow leopard, and the clouded leopard. Outside of the tropical rain forests, they are among the botanically richest sites of the world and are home to between 5,000 and 6,000 species of flora. It has been noted that the region is similar to the Paleotropical forests of the Tertiary Period.

SHOPPING AND EATING IN CHINA

As China is now the largest manufacturer in the world, shopping in China is an experience not to be missed. Most large and distinctive Chinese cities— such as Beijing, Shanghai, Xi'an, Hangzhou, and Guangzhou—feature special business streets, where local products are on sale and haggling is possible. There are also large Western department stores, such as Carrefour and Walmart. In addition, there is delicious Chinese cuisine to savor. Chinese delicacies vary widely from region to region due to available resources, climate, geography, history, cooking techniques, and lifestyle. In general, the Chinese favor stir-frying as a way to maximize available heat and plenty of garlic, shallots, and spices to flavor their food. They also love noodles—one can find them in all shapes and sizes.

GEOGRAPHY

The steep limestone karst mountains of Wulingyuan in Hunan.

T HE MIDDLE KINGDOM, AS CHINA IS known to the Chinese, sits in East Asia and covers an area of 3.7 million square miles (9.6 million square km).

China borders 15 countries. The 9,010-mile (14,500-km) coastline touches the Bohai, Yellow, East, and South China seas. China has more than 5,000 islands—in its territorial seas. China's extensive territorial waters are principally marginal seas of the western Pacific Ocean.

MOUNTAINOUS TERRAIN

China's landmass consists mainly of mountains, plateaus, and deserts. Of the total landmass, only 14.9 percent can be used for agriculture to feed the country's 1.3 billion people. It is, therefore, a feat that China grows enough food to feed its own people and to export to other countries. In the southwest is the Tibetan plateau, the world's highest highland at 13,500 feet (4,115 m). Bordering the plateau in the south are the Himalayas, including Mount Everest, called Zhumulangma Feng by the Chinese, on the China-Nepal border.

DESERTS AND PLAINS

Elevations drop to between 6,560 and 3,280 feet (1,999 and 1,000 m) toward the famous grasslands of Mongolia and the Gobi Desert.

In the northwest is the Taklimakan Desert, the largest in China, through which the ancient Silk Road once passed. The government has constructed a cross-desert highway that links the cities of Hotan (on the southern edge) and Luntai (on the northern edge). North of the desert is

Geographically China is the third-largest country in the world, slightly larger than the United States. China spans 3,123 miles (5,026 km) from east to west and 4,320 miles (6,952 km) from north to south.

the Tian Shan range. The latter stands between two great basins, the massive Tarim Basin to the south and the Dzungarian Basin to the north. Rich deposits of coal, oil, and metallic ores lie in the Tian Shan area. The largest inland basin in China, the Tarim Basin measures 932 miles (1,500 km) from east to west and 373 miles (600 km) from north to south at its widest parts. The Turpan Basin, an oasis at the northern edge of the Taklimakan Desert, is the lowest point in China at 505 feet (154 m) below sea level, where temperatures can reach 120°F (48.9°C).

In the southern provinces, the terrain changes to unusually shaped cliffs, gorges, and waterfalls.

Toward the coast in the east, elevations drop to around 1,500 feet (457 m). This area is the Great Plains region of China and the focus of agriculture and human settlement.

China's major rivers help to shape the coastline as they carry silt toward the sea. The Yellow River carries 1.4 billion tons (1.27 billion metric tons) of silt to the sea annually, but since 1996 its river delta has been reported to be shrinking slightly each year due to erosion from currents from the sea.

CLIMATE

Most of China has a temperate climate, but with striking extremes: harsh northern Siberian frosts, arid western deserts, and lush tropical weather in the southeast. Monsoon winds, caused by differences in the heat-absorbing capacity of the continent and the ocean dominate the climate. Alternating seasonal air-mass movements and accompanying winds are moist in summer and dry in winter. The advance and retreat of the monsoons account in large degree for the timing of the rainy season and the amount of rainfall throughout the country. Although China spans five time zones, the whole country follows the same time as its capital, Beijing.

Northern winters are bitter cold, with temperatures dropping to −104°F (−76°C). In the northern city of Harbin it is cold enough for a winter-long exhibition of ice sculptures. Provinces in the north and the northwest may experience extreme weather conditions within a single day—freezing cold in

The Gobi Desert near the Mogao Caves.

The size of the Gobi Desert has increased and now reaches the outskirts of Beijing.

the morning, hot by midday. Springtime in the north brings sandstorms from Mongolia, blowing fine sand everywhere, even through the tiniest cracks in buildings.

China is officially divided into north and south by the Yangtze River. As the south is warmer than the north, people in cities south of the river do not have central heating in their buildings. In winter it is not surprising to find residents of cities just south of the river bundled up to keep warm. In the Yangtze River Delta near the coast, the weather is warm and humid with four distinct seasons. Here winters are much shorter, with the average temperature around 50°F (10°C).

Summers in the north can be as punishing as winters. Temperatures can reach highs of 100°F (37.8°C) or more. Fall is cool and dry.

WATERWAYS

YANGTZE RIVER Also known as Changjiang, or Long River, the Yangtze rises in the Qinghai-Tibetan Mountains. Measuring 3,988 miles (6,418 km),

The Yellow River.

it is the longest river in China and the third-longest in the world. It flows through nine provinces, emptying into the East China Sea near Shanghai.

The Yangtze has 700 tributaries and flows through important industrial and agricultural areas. Half of China's crops are grown in the Yangtze Delta, especially rice, the country's staple food. The Three Gorges Dam on the Yangtze River is the largest hydroelectric power station in the world. A stretch of the Yangtze flowing through deep gorges in western Yunnan is part of the Three Parallel Rivers of Yunnan Protected Areas, a UNESCO World Heritage Site.

YELLOW RIVER The Huang He, or Yellow River, starts as melting snow in the Qinghai-Tibetan Mountains. Its 3,395-mile (5,464-km) journey traverses nine provinces before it empties into the Bohai Sea. As it flows through the central Loess Plateau, it picks up an incredible amount of loose yellow soil, which gives the river its name.

The Huang He has been called "China's sorrow," for it has flooded its banks more than a thousand times, destroying crops and killing countless people. A total of 1 billion tons (910 million metric tons) of silt carried downstream each year make the Huang He the muddiest river in the world. The riverbed rises by 4 inches (10 cm) annually, overflowing its banks. The silt buildup has over the centuries caused the river to change course 12 times. Near its estuary, the water is so thick and low that there is little marine life.

The Huang He is also known as the cradle of Chinese civilization, for it was along the fertile banks of this river that land in China was first cultivated.

THE GRAND CANAL

The Grand Canal is the oldest and longest man-made canal in China. The earliest parts were dug in the fifth century B.C. This 1,105-mile (1,778-km) canal was an immense project in terms of labor and lives lost.

During the Sui Dynasty (A.D. 581—618) the then-capital of Luoyang was linked to the old capital of Xi'an. With the recorded labor of 5 million men and women under the supervision of overseer Ma Shumou, the first major section of the Grand Canal, called the Bian Qu, was completed in the year 605. The second stage of the Grand Canal was completed under the second Sui emperor, in 609, first by linking Luoyang to the city of Yangzhou (and the Yangtze Valley), then by expanding it to Hangzhou in the south and Beijing in the north. After the canal's completion, Emperor Yang led a recorded 65-mile-long (105-km-long) naval flotilla from the north down to his southern capital at Yangzhou.

The main function of the canal was to move troops in times of war, but it was also used for the transportation of food from the fertile south to the barren north. This gradually made the south the agricultural center of China. In addition to its function as a grain shipment route and major vein of river-borne indigenous trade in China, the Grand Canal had long been a government-operated courier route. During the Ming Dynasty, official courier stations were placed at intervals of 21.7 miles—28 miles (35—45 km).

The Grand Canal connects four major rivers—the Huang He, the Yangtze, the Huai, and the Qiantang. It passes through some of the prettiest parts of China.

Much of the canal has fallen into disuse due to the construction of road and railway links and the repeated flooding of the Huang He. The Grand Canal nominally runs between Beijing and Hangzhou over a length of 1,115 miles (1,794 km). However, only the section from Hangzhou to Jining is currently navigable, mainly for the transportation of agricultural products and raw materials to factories and warehouses. It is also used to irrigate the drought-prone areas of Hubei, Henan, and Anhui provinces. The economic importance of the canal will likely increase because the governments of Shandong, Jiangsu, and Zhejiang provinces have implemented a dredging program that should increase shipping capacity by 40 percent by 2012.

The Grand Canal is currently being upgraded to serve as the Eastern Route of the South-North Water Transfer Project. Construction on the Eastern Route officially began on December 27, 2002, and water was supposed to reach Tianjin by 2012. However, water pollution has affected the viability of this project.

From these beginnings, villages, towns, and empires grew. Major floods in A.D. 11 are said to be the reason for the fall of the shortlived Xin Dynasty (A.D. 9—23), when the river once more changed its course from the north, near Tianjin, to the south of the Shandong Peninsula.

PEARL RIVER The name Pearl River is usually used to refer to the watersheds of the Xi Jiang (West River), the Bei Jiang (North River), and the Dong Jiang (East River). These rivers are all considered tributaries of the Pearl River because they share the Pearl River Delta. This 1,367-mile (2,200-km) river drains the majority of Guangdong and Guangxi provinces and is one of the world's most polluted waterways.

CITIES

BEIJING Beijing is China's capital. It is China's political, economic, scientific, and cultural center and contains some of the country's finest buildings as well as palaces.

In the center of Beijing is Tiananmen Square. The largest public square in the world, it can hold up to 1 million people. On the northern side is the Tiananmen Gate, the Gate of Heavenly Peace, which was once used as the main gate to the Ming and Qing imperial palaces; today visitors use this gate as the entrance to the Forbidden City. From this gate, on October 1, 1949, Mao Zedong proclaimed the founding of the People's Republic of China. During the Qing Dynasty, the square was enclosed by a red wall, and commoners entered it only to be executed.

China's capital city of Beijing.

With a population of about 19.6 million people, this bustling commercial city with its numerous foreign embassies is also the seat of government. China's 23 provinces, five autonomous regions, four municipalities, and two special administrative regions (SARs) are administered from Beijing.

Beijing was host to the 2008 Summer Olympic Games. The Beijing National Stadium, one of 31 venues built for the event, was dubbed "the Bird's Nest" because of its nestlike skeletal structure. To prepare for Olympic visitors, Beijing's transportation infrastructure was expanded significantly. Beijing's airport underwent a major renovation with the addition of Terminal 3, the world's second-largest airport terminal, designed by the renowned architect Norman Foster.

The 2008 Summer Olympics emblem was known as Dancing Beijing. The emblem combined a traditional Chinese red seal and a representation of

This famous complex of buildings in Beijing is called the Forbidden City because at one time only the emperor and his court could live there. This cluster of imperial palaces was built in 1406-1420, during the Ming Dynasty. It is surrounded by a wide moat and a high wall. There are 9,999 rooms. If a newborn prince lived in a different room every day of his life, he would be 27 years old by the time he had slept in them all!

The area around the Forbidden City is equally interesting. Still standing are medieval buildings that once held businesses catering to the needs of the people in nearby palaces. In fact, the imperial pharmacy is still in business and dispenses the same kind of pills and potions that used to cure princes; the royal shoe shop is not far off.

the calligraphic character jing (京, "national capital," also the second character of Beijing's Chinese name) with athletic features. The open arms of the calligraphic word symbolized the invitation from China to the world to share in its culture.

The opening ceremony officially began at 8:00 P.M. local time on August 8, 2008, in the Beijing National Stadium. The number eight is associated with prosperity and confidence in Chinese culture, and here it was a triple eight for the date and one extra for time. The ceremony was codirected by Chinese filmmaker Zhang Yimou and Chinese choreographer Zhang Jigang and featured more than 15,000 performers. The ceremony lasted more than four hours and was reported to have cost more than $100 million to produce.

SHANGHAI Shanghai sits at the meeting point of two rivers: the Huangpu and the Wusong. The city has always been an important port in China and today handles the country's largest amount of freight annually. Located at the heart of the Yangtze River Delta, Shanghai has the world's busiest container port, which handled 29.05 million twenty-foot equivalent units (TEUs) in 2010.

In the mid-19th century, after the Opium Wars, Shanghai opened its doors to the West. Foreign banks, shops, and embassies were built, all with a distinct European flavor. The Shanghainese were exposed to a more Western lifestyle and thought themselves more sophisticated than other Chinese. Shanghai was once called the "Paris of the East," and the style of the mid-19th century can be seen in the old buildings.

Shanghai is one of China's most densely populated cities, with about 23 million inhabitants. Based on the population of its total administrative area, Shanghai is the second-largest of the four direct-controlled municipalities of the People's Republic of China, behind Chongqing, which governs an area more than 10 times larger than that of Shanghai. Numerous foreign entrepreneurs and technicians have settled in Shanghai, strengthening its claim to be China's most international metropolis. Today Shanghai is again one of the most prosperous cities in the world. Its cosmopolitan character, sophisticated and affluent consumers, and highly educated skilled labor force make it very attractive to overseas investors. Shanghai recorded double-digit growth every year since 1992, except during the global recession of 2008 and 2009, to become the center of finance and trade in China.

The Shanghai Disneyland Resort was approved by the government on November 4, 2009. It is currently under construction. The resort is planned to be operational by 2013. The $4.4 billion theme park and resort in the Pudong area of Shanghai will have a castle that will be the biggest among Disney's resorts.

GUANGZHOU Guangzhou (formerly Canton) is the capital of Guangdong Province. It is one of the most ancient Chinese cities, with a history that goes back 20 centuries. Legend says that five gods came riding into the city on five rams. Each brought a six-ear rice plant so that the town would forever be free of famine. The gods vanished, and the rams turned into stone. Today there is a sculpture of five rams in the city, which is still known as the City of Rams.

Guangzhou sits on the fertile Pearl River Delta, facing the South China Sea. Because of its position, it was visited by Indians as far back as the second century A.D., and it is now an important trading and industrial city and one of the most modern and enterprising places in China. Guangzhou is the main manufacturing hub of the Pearl River Delta, one of mainland China's leading commercial and manufacturing regions. In 2009 its gross domestic product (GDP) reached ¥911.28 billion ($133.5 billion).

Cantonese is the first language for half of the 14 million residents of Guangzhou, while the other half speak mainly Mandarin. Being in the far south of China, Guangzhou is warm and moist almost all year long. It has lush green vegetation, abundant rice fields, and fruit orchards.

Guangzhou's subway network is made up of eight lines, covering a total length of 147 miles (236 km). A long-term plan is to expand the system by more than 310 miles (500 km) by 2020, with 15 lines in operation. Currently Guangzhou has more vehicles fueled by liquefied petroleum gas (LPG), a more environmentally friendly fuel, than any other city in the world. On January 1, 2007, the municipal government banned motorcycles in urban areas to reduce congestion and pollution.

FLORA AND FAUNA

China's plant life includes nearly all species of plants found in the frigid and temperate zones. Plants that existed in the Ice Age have been found growing in some hidden corners of the country. Forests are filled with cypress, pine, and bamboo. There are also hundreds of varieties of chrysanthemum and peony. There are more than 32,000 species of plants and 2,500 species of forest trees in China. The diversity of plants includes living fossils, such as the ginkgo tree, whose imprints have been found in rocks as old as 270 million years.

China's range of wildlife is equally impressive. There are 400 species of mammals, 1,300 species of birds, 424 species of reptiles, and 300 species of amphibians. China's massive population of 1.3 billion people poses a constant threat to the natural environment. There are more than 100 species of rare endangered animals, including the giant panda, the golden monkey, the Manchurian tiger, and the snow leopard. One reason for the endangered status of some species could be the Chinese culinary habits, as snakes are

THE GIANT PANDA

The giant panda, China's favorite animal, is threatened with extinction. Pandas live on a diet of only bamboo leaves. With urbanization, more bamboo plants are being destroyed, forcing the pandas to go higher up into the mountains in search of food. Unfortunately, many pandas die of starvation due to the shrinking bamboo forests. The average giant panda eats as much as 20 to 30 pounds (9—14 kg) of bamboo shoots a day. Initially the primary method of breeding giant pandas in captivity was by artificial insemination, as they seemed to lose their interest in mating once they were captured. This led some scientists to try extreme methods such as showing them videos of giant pandas mating and giving the males Viagra.

served in abundance in Chinese restaurants. In fact, an estimated 10,000 tons (9,072 metric tons) of serpents are delivered to restaurants, or to put it bluntly, eaten, every year. This has led to 43 of China's 200 snake species being endangered. The reduction in the number of snakes led to an increase in rodent numbers, which was disastrous for crops.

As of 2007, China had 2,531 nature reserves covering 14.7 percent of China's total land area.

INTERNET LINKS

http://china.mrdonn.org/geography.html

This website encompasses a comprehensive list of stories, games, geography, and maps of China for young readers.

http://encyclopedia.kids.net.au/page/ge/Geography_of_China

This website provides fascinating facts on the geography of China.

http://kids.nationalgeographic.com/kids/places/find/china/

This is a fun web page full of interesting facts and pictures about China.

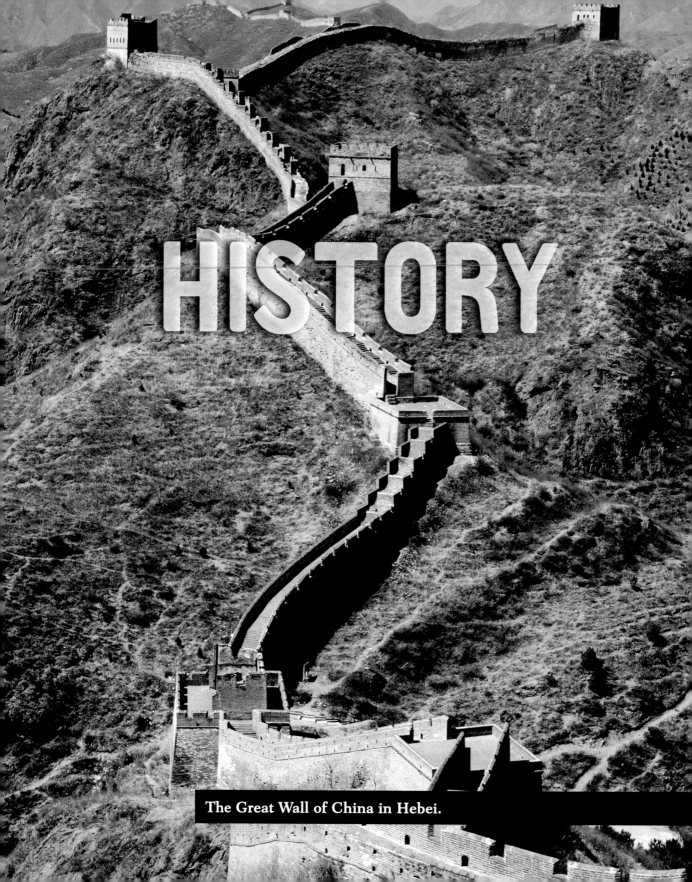

HISTORY

The Great Wall of China in Hebei.

M ORE THAN A HALF-MILLION years ago, primitive human beings lived in China. Evidence of *Homo erectus*, estimated to be around 420,000 years old, was first found near Beijing in the 1920s.

These fossils included partial skeletal remains, stone tools, and animal bones. In 1929 the first complete skull was discovered, the remains of what is now known as Peking Man. The site of the remains, Zhoukoudian, is 30 miles (48 km) southwest of Beijing.

THE FIRST DYNASTY

Accounts of the legendary period before the 22nd century B.C. mingle fact and fiction—rulers were immortal, and dragons and other mythical creatures such as phoenixes and griffins prowled the earth. At this time there arose the Xia Dynasty (2205—1766 B.C.). Archaeological evidence indicates that the Xia were descended from a Neolithic culture, based in the Yellow River Valley, called Longshan, famous for its black-lacquered pottery. The Xia were overthrown by the Shang (1766—1123 B.C.).

SHANG AND ZHOU DYNASTIES

Records of daily life in urban societies during the Shang Dynasty have been found carved on bones, tortoise shells, and bronze.

The Shang were conquered by the Zhou, who ruled by a feudal system in which leaders of the different states of the empire swore loyalty and paid taxes to the emperor.

2

The Chinese people have shared a common culture longer than any other group on earth. The Chinese writing system, for example, dates back almost 4,000 years.

The discovery of iron casting during this period resulted in improved farm tools and the development of large-scale irrigation. The resulting prosperity made China one of the most advanced civilizations in the world at that time. Also during this time Taoism and Confucianism evolved, introducing ideas that are still evident in Chinese thinking today.

After 200 years of peace, the Zhou Dynasty disintegrated into smaller squabbling states (Spring and Autumn Period) that later grouped into larger states (Warring States Period).

QIN SHI HUANG

China was truly united for the first time under (ruled 221—206 B.C.), or "the first exalted emperor." He ascended the throne of the state of Qin at the age of 13 and went on to conquer the surrounding states. He completed his conquest of the other states in 221 B.C. As the first emperor, he is remembered for both the great and the terrible things he did.

The terra-cotta warriors of Qin Shi Huang.

Qin Shi Huang abolished the feudal system and established a new order of society that was to last for 2,000 years. People were divided into different classes: aristocrats, landowners, bureaucrats, peasants, merchants, and slaves.

The emperor set up a central government, and he recruited the best scholars as civil servants. This stressed the importance of learning, raised the level of education and culture, and made China a nation ruled by scholars. In addition, a style of writing well suited for the compilation of official documents was developed. The first Chinese dictionary was compiled in A.D. 100. Containing more than 9,000 words, it explained the meanings of the words and provided examples of the various forms of the words used in writing.

Qin Shi Huang also standardized the written language, the system of weights and measures, and a form of currency. Transportation links to the capital, such as roads and canals, were built.

THE GREAT WALL

The Great Wall, symbol of China's ancient civilization, stretches for 5,500 miles (8,851 km) across northern China. Its construction started during the Spring and Autumn Period (770—476 B.C.). Rival feudal kingdoms built walls around their territories to keep out invading nomadic tribes from the north. When Qin Shi Huang unified China, he began to link up and extend these walls.

Prisoners of war, convicts, soldiers, civilians, and farmers labored to build the Great Wall. Millions died of starvation, disease, and exhaustion during the construction. Their bodies were buried in the foundations or used as part of the wall. Any materials found nearby—clay, stone, willow branches, reeds, and sand—were used.

The Great Wall crosses loess plateaus, mountains, deserts, rivers, and valleys, passing through five provinces and two autonomous regions. It is about 20 feet (6 m) wide and 26 feet (8 m) high. Parts of the wall are so broad that 10 soldiers can walk abreast.

Parts of the old wall can still be seen in remote parts of China. Most visitors see the portions that were restored during the Ming Dynasty, when stone slabs replaced clay bricks. The wall took 100 years to rebuild, and it is said that the amount of material used in the present wall alone is enough to circle the world at the equator five times.

Contrary to popular belief, astronauts cannot see the Great Wall of China from the moon. The apparent width of the Great Wall from the moon is the same as that of a human hair viewed from 2 miles (3.2 km) away.

A shrewd and jealous man, Qin Shi Huang is said to have buried alive hundreds of scholars whose views were different from his or who appeared to be smarter than he was. He also burned thousands of books for the same reason. Precious works of great philosophers such as Confucius and Mencius were destroyed; what we read now was rewritten from memory by scholars.

In 1974, farmers digging a well in Xi'an discovered a vault containing 6,000 life-size terra-cotta warriors depicted in full uniform and arranged in battle formation protecting Qin Shi Huang's nearby tomb. It is now a UNESCO site and one of the most popular tourist attractions in China.

HAN DYNASTY

The Han Dynasty (206 B.C.—A.D. 220) was one of the most important dynasties to rule China. Established after the overthrow of Qin Shi Huang, the Han Dynasty was of such significance that even today the Chinese refer to themselves as "men of Han."

There were many notable achievements during Han rule. Trade flourished, and China was opened to other cultures. The legendary Silk Road was well traveled, and contacts were made with Central and West Asia and even with Rome.

Buddhism was introduced from India, and Confucianism became the state doctrine. A thorough knowledge of Confucian classics became essential for officials and candidates for the civil service. Painting and other arts also flourished, and many historical and philosophical works were written.

Advancements were made in science and technology. Water clocks and sundials were used by officials. Paper was invented and a seismograph developed.

The Han Dynasty lasted for more than 400 years. Eventually a succession of corrupt and weak rulers led to its downfall.

NORTHERN WEI DYNASTY

The Northern Wei Dynasty ruled northern China from 386 to 534. It is perhaps most noted for the unification of northern China in 439 but was also a period when foreign ideas were introduced, and Buddhism became firmly established. Many antiques and artworks, both Taoist and Buddhist, from this period have survived.

DYNASTIC TRANSITION

For the next 400 years China was divided into separate kingdoms constantly fighting for power. The nomadic tribes from the north succeeded for a while in gaining a foothold in China. Following the Han Dynasty were the

The Han Dynasty was founded by Liu Bang, a rebel peasant who once urinated into the hat of a court scholar to show his disdain for education. Nevertheless he later proved himself a practical and flexible ruler and had learned men in his court.

The ancient Silk Road was established some 2,000 years ago. Starting at Chang'an, the ancient capital (present-day Xi'an), it stretched westward for 4,350 miles (7,000 km), crossing mountains and deserts all the way to the eastern coast of the Mediterranean. From there, trade goods were taken to Constantinople (present-day Istanbul, Turkey) and Rome.

Chinese silk and other Chinese inventions, such as paper, printing from wood blocks, gunpowder, and the compass, made their way to East Asia, the Middle East, and Europe along this route. In turn, merchants introduced foreign religions, art, and cultures to China. They also brought agricultural products, and the Chinese soon began eating grapes, walnuts, cucumbers, broad beans, and watermelon. Silk was also exchanged for Persian horses, glass, perfume, and ivory.

Merchants traveled the Silk Road on camels. Chosen because of their docile temper and their endurance of the sun and sand, these animals carried enormous loads across mountains and deserts. But few people traveled the entire span of the road; goods were passed from one middleman to another along the route.

Later, with the loss of Roman territory in Asia, the Silk Road became overrun by bandits, and few people traveled it. In the 13th and 14th centuries, the Mongol rulers of China revived the use of the road by which Marco Polo, the Italian merchant-adventurer, arrived in Mongol-ruled China.

the Three Kingdoms and the Western Jin, the Eastern Jin, the Northern and Southern, and the Sui dynasties. The Sui Dynasty went bankrupt because of large expansion programs in public works and expeditions to Central Asia. Nevertheless, the Sui Dynasty laid the groundwork for the greatest Chinese dynasty, the Tang.

TANG DYNASTY

The Tang Dynasty lasted almost 300 years, from 618 to 907, during which time Central Asia, Korea, and northern Vietnam came under China's rule.

THE FOUR GREAT INVENTIONS OF ANCIENT CHINA

Many things that we take for granted in everyday life were invented in China. For example, the umbrella, eyeglasses, paper money, the kite, the mechanical clock, and even the washboard made their way to the West after being developed in China. The four most important inventions from ancient China were paper, printing, gunpowder, and the compass.

PAPER *Paper is believed to have been invented by Chai Lun (or Ts'ai Lun) around A.D. 105. Before paper was invented, the Chinese carved characters on bone and tortoiseshell. Later, the first book was bound using strips of bamboo held together with string. People then started writing on silk, which proved too expensive.*

Paper first made its appearance during the Han Dynasty. Bark, bits of hemp, cloth, and old fishing nets were boiled to a pulp. This pulp was rinsed, pounded flat, and spread out on fine bamboo screens to form sheets of paper.

PRINTING *At first, each printing block contained an entire page of text, so each block could only be used to produce that same page of a book. During the Song Dynasty, single characters were engraved on individual blocks of wood. Each block could then be used repeatedly. Assembled to form sentences and pages, they were inked, and moistened paper was placed over them.*

GUNPOWDER *During the period of the Warring States, alchemists trying to make immortality pills discovered that a mixture of sulfur and saltpeter caused an explosion when heated. At first, the new discovery was used for firecrackers. Later gunpowder was used in war for the first time during the Tang Dynasty. Firecrackers are still lit in China during Chinese New Year.*

COMPASS *The compass was first used more than 2,000 years ago when the Chinese discovered that a piece of natural magnetite would automatically point in a north-south direction. The Chinese soon started to fashion magnets of ingenious design.*

One was of a wooden figure on a horse-drawn chariot, and no matter which direction the chariot turned, the figure would always be pointing north.

Compasses became common as navigational devices on ships between 850 and 1050.

The Tang Dynasty is considered the golden age of Chinese history and art. Improvements to agriculture and farming tools increased food production. Government administration was in the hands of top Confucian scholars. Chinese literature and other arts flourished, and the art of printing was developed.

Although Tang rule gradually deteriorated, no subsequent dynasty matched the impact of the Tang on China. Many dynasties that followed were modeled on the Tang Dynasty in the hope of reaching the same heights of glory. None did.

SONG DYNASTY

The Song Dynasty was a ruling dynasty in China between 960 and 1279. It was the first government in world history to issue banknotes, or paper money, and the first Chinese government to establish a permanent standing navy. This dynasty also saw the first known use of gunpowder, as well as first discernment of true north using a compass. The population of China doubled in size during the 10th and 11th centuries. This growth came through expanded rice cultivation in central and southern China, the use of early-ripening rice from southeast and southern Asia, and the production of abundant food surpluses. This dramatic increase of population fomented an economic revolution in premodern China. The expansion of the population was partially the cause for the gradual withdrawal of the central government from heavily regulating the market economy.

The East Lake of Shaoxing is a man-made lake that was created during the Qing Dynasty.

THE LAST DYNASTY

China came under imperial rule for the last time in 1644 when the Ming Dynasty was overthrown by Manchurians from the north.

The Qing Dynasty (1644–1911) lasted 267 years, ruling over territory that included Manchuria, Tibet, Taiwan, and Turkestan (now Xinjiang). The empire had never been larger. For the first 150 years, the country was well run and prospered under able emperors. Success gave way to power struggles among corrupt court officials.

Few Europeans traveled in China, as only the port of Canton (now Guangzhou) was open to them. They came to buy Chinese goods, such as tea, silk, and porcelain, but they could not sell anything, as China was largely self-sufficient. To balance the trade, the British started selling opium to the Chinese in the 1780s. The Qing government tried to ban its sale, but corrupt officials and merchants did nothing to stop it. This soon led to a series of wars known as the Opium Wars, in which the Chinese were defeated by the British and their society devastated.

In submitting to British demands in the Treaty of Nanking (1842), the Qing government granted land to the British and allowed them to open several more ports to trade. Hong Kong became a British colony. Other European nations also forced the Qing government to sign similar treaties.

China was soon in debt and its people heavily taxed. Soon the Taiping Rebellion broke out in the south. The Taiping Rebellion was a widespread civil war in southern China from 1850 to 1864. Heterodox Christian convert Hong Xiuquan, who, having received visions, maintained that he was the younger brother of Jesus Christ, led the forces against the Qing government. About 20 million people, mainly civilians, died in one of the deadliest military conflicts in history. This weakened the government even more, and Britain, France, and Russia took the opportunity to occupy even more Chinese land. The Qing Dynasty finally collapsed in 1911.

MODERN CHINA

Sun Yat-sen, leader of the Kuomintang (Nationalist Party), or KMT, established the Republic of China in 1912 and became its president. The new republic was not at peace, however, as partisans in various parts of the country fought for power. One in particular, Yuan Shikai, a former Qing minister, controlled much of northern China. In order to keep the peace, Sun gave up the presidency to Yuan.

Yuan declared himself emperor in 1915 and made Beijing his capital. He died in 1916 after being in power for just three weeks, and China was back in the hands of partisans. From the south, Sun Yat-sen tried to fight the partisans and arouse national support, but he was unsuccessful.

Sun Yat-sen was the leader of China's Kuomintang.

In 1919, at the Paris Peace Conference that ended World War I, the German concessions in Shandong were handed over to Japan instead of being returned to the Chinese. This sparked off the May Fourth Movement. Workers and intellectuals boycotted Japanese goods and demonstrated against foreign intervention, as well as all things connected with feudal China.

What started out as a protest at Beijing University spread to every part of the country and became a national movement toward modernization. These demonstrations sparked national protests and marked the beginning of Chinese nationalism.

NATIONALISTS AND COMMUNISTS   When Sun Yat-sen died in 1925, his colleague Chiang Kai-shek took over. Chiang succeeded in unifying China by defeating the partisans in the north. He made Nanjing his capital.

Chiang then began to fight the communists, who had formed a political party in 1921. Mao Zedong was one of the founder members of the Chinese Communist Party (CCP). In 1923, the Chiang-led Kuomintang and the CCP allied to combat the warlords that controlled much of northern China. Subsequently, in 1927, the KMT turned against its former allies and drove the communists into the southern mountains.

In October 1934, led by Mao, the communists began a heroic journey known as the Long March. Traveling 7,767 miles (12,500 km) on foot over some of the harshest parts of the country, they arrived in Shaanxi in the northwest and set up their headquarters there in 1935. Of the 200,000 people who began the Long March from Jiangxi, only 8,000 made it to Shaanxi Province.

Chiang Kai-shek, determined to eliminate the communists, overlooked the danger presented by Japanese troops moving into China. Even when the Sino-Japanese War began in 1937, Chiang went on fighting the communists.

Two of Chiang's own generals finally arrested him and forced him to make an alliance with the communists to fight the Japanese, who had occupied eastern China. By the end of World War II in 1945, the Japanese, defeated by the Americans in the Pacific, moved out of China.

As both sides fought to gain control of China, civil war broke out between the Kuomintang and the Communist Party. The Communist People's

Liberation Army (PLA), which had the support of the peasants, defeated the nationalists in 1949. In 1950 the Kuomintang fled to Taiwan, and it has since ruled the island as the Republic of China.

THE PEOPLE'S REPUBLIC OF CHINA

On October 1, 1949, Mao Zedong declared the founding of the People's Republic of China. China was in economic trouble after so many years of fighting wars. The Communist Party had not only to establish a new political system but also to revive the economy and put it on par with those of other countries. By 1953 the economy had recovered considerably. Encouraged by this success, Mao Zedong launched a campaign in 1958 known as the Great Leap Forward.

THE GREAT LEAP FORWARD The countryside was divided into communes, with 5,000 households in each, so that labor was used effectively. Everyone ate in a communal hall, children were looked after in boarding schools, and adults worked in fields and factories. Crop yields increased, and industrial output such as steel production went up by as much as 50 percent.

Spurred by this success, the government took more peasants out of the fields to work in factories. Agriculture began to suffer, however, and the peasants were exhausted. Then floods and droughts drove the country into famine. The campaign was aborted in 1960, and Mao was forced to take a backseat as some party members—including the secretary-general of the party, Deng Xiaoping—began to get the economy into shape again.

THE CULTURAL REVOLUTION In 1966 Mao tried to regain control by starting the Cultural Revolution. Claiming that China was threatened by capitalism, he called for a rebellion against the Four Olds—old ideas, old culture, old habits, and old customs. China was caught up in a frenzy of destruction. Books were burned, relics destroyed, and temples torn down. Homes of intellectuals and people suspected of harboring the Four Olds were smashed, and they and their families were thrown into prison or sent to the countryside to work. Among these was Deng Xiaoping.

Mao Zedong led the People's Republic of China from 1949 until his death in 1976.

China's recovery from this calamity was ably accomplished by the respected premier Zhou Enlai, who worked to repair the damage to the economy. Both Zhou Enlai and Mao Zedong died in 1976, and the Cultural Revolution ended. Deng Xiaoping won the ensuing power struggle.

China under Deng Xiaoping underwent radical reform. Economic packages introduced in 1979 helped the country prosper, and China opened its doors to foreign travelers and businesses. Nevertheless, political problems persisted. In June 1989 clashes in Tiananmen Square between students demonstrating for democracy and the PLA resulted in numerous deaths.

AFTER TIANANMEN There was a significant impact on the Chinese economy after the Tiananmen Square demonstration. Foreign loans to China were suspended by the World Bank, the Asian Development Bank, and world governments; tourism revenue decreased from $2.2 billion to $1.8 billion; foreign direct investment commitments were canceled; and defense spending rose from 8.6 percent in 1986 to 15.5 percent in 1990, reversing a previous 10-year decline. The continuance of economic reform led to economic growth in the 1990s, which allowed the government to regain much of the support it had lost in 1989.

Under the leadership of Jiang Zemin, China experienced substantial developmental growth with reforms, saw the peaceful return of Hong Kong from the United Kingdom and of Macau from Portugal, and improved its relations with the outside world while the Communist Party maintained its tight control over the government.

Jiang did not specialize in economics, and in 1997 he handed most of the economic governance of the country to Zhu Rongji, who remained in office through the Asian financial crisis. Under their joint leadership, China sustained an average annual GDP growth of 10 percent, the highest rate of per capita economic growth among major world economies. This was achieved mostly by continuing the process of a transition to a market economy.

Jiang Zemin was succeeded by Hu Jintao as general secretary of the Communist Party on November 15, 2002. Along with his colleague in charge of the economy, Wen Jiabao, Hu has presided over nearly a decade of consistent economic growth and development that has cemented China as a major world power. Through Hu's tenure, China's global influence in Africa, Latin America, and other developing areas has increased.

General Secretary Hu and Premier Wen inherited a China wrought with internal social, political, and environmental problems. One of the biggest challenges Hu faces is the large wealth disparity between the Chinese rich and poor, along with the favoritism and corruption plaguing China's civil service, military, educational, judicial, and medical systems. For all the challenges he faces, Hu was named the 2010 World's Most Powerful Person by *Forbes* magazine.

INTERNET LINKS

http://china.mrdonn.org/dynasties.html

This website provides stories and games for kids about the history of China.

www.historyforkids.org/learn/china/history/index.htm

This website provides a comprehensive account of the history of China through attractive pictures and numerous hyperlinks. This site also has lots of book recommendations.

www.kidspast.com/world-history/0125-civilization-in-china.php

This website furnishes an easy-to-understand summary of civilizations in China from its origins 5,000 years ago.

GOVERNMENT

The entrance to the Great Hall of the People at Tiananmen Square.

3

CHINA HAS BEEN RULED BY the Chinese Communist Party (CCP) since 1949.

Founded in July 1921, its policies and beliefs on paper are based on the ideas of Marxism-Leninism combined with Mao Zedong Thought, which hinges on the notion that the highest phase of human society should be a communist one, where properties are owned by all and there are no socio-economic classes. China is a single-party, bureaucratic, authoritarian state in which capitalism is allowed to flourish, but many rights that are considered basic in democracies are denied. Blending imperial Chinese traditions, Confucianism, and China's unique take on communism, the ruling regime has near-complete control over the government.

China's constitution provides for the CCP's operation alongside other parties, but there are no truly independent parties. National political activity is managed by the CCP through its members in high-level government offices. Political activities differing from the CCP's objectives are restricted, hampering the rise of any significant opposition. The system of government is essentially one-party rule.

The Chinese government has an unwritten agreement with the Chinese people that it can remain in power as long as it brings prosperity to the people. It seems to have done this by buying off the elite with business deals and opportunities to make money; placating the middle class with apartments, cars, and travel; and raising hopes among the poor with chances to seek a better life. The Chinese people are now enjoying the fruits of economic growth instead of their historical sufferings.

GOVERNMENT HIERARCHY

THE PRESIDENT AND THE VICE PRESIDENT The president is the official head of state. The vice president takes his place when the president is

A poll conducted by the Pew Research Center before the 2008 Olympics found that 86 percent of the Chinese interviewed were happy with the direction that China was going, up from 48 percent in 2002, and two-thirds thought the government was doing a good job. Approval ratings of the government have increased as the economy has improved, but the people surveyed did have issues with corruption, environmental problems, and inflation.

unable to perform formal duties. The president's office is mainly ceremonial, and power lies with the Communist Party's general secretary, a post that the current president also holds.

The primary leadership positions in China are the president, the general secretary of the Communist Party, and the chairman of the Central Military Commission, the de facto head of the military.

THE NPC The National People's Congress (NPC) is the highest organ of state power in China, with the power to amend the constitution and make laws. It also elects the president, the vice president, the chairman of the Central Military Commission, the president of the Supreme People's Court, and the procurator-general, and it approves the nomination of the premier by the president and the members of the State Council. The NPC is made up of deputies elected from the provinces, autonomous regions, and municipalities. It meets once a year in Beijing to decide on major issues affecting the country.

THE STATE COUNCIL The State Council enforces the laws and decisions of the NPC and has the power to adopt administrative measures and issue orders. It is made up of the premier, the vice premiers, state councillors, ministers, the auditor general, and the secretary-general. The premier has overall responsibility for and directs the work of the State Council.

THE CENTRAL MILITARY COMMISSION Headed by a chairman, the Central Military Commission commands the PLA, the People's Armed Police Force, and the militia. It is accountable to the NPC.

THE SUPREME PEOPLE'S COURT AND THE PEOPLE'S PROCURATORATE The people's courts and procuratorates try criminal and civil cases and uphold China's legal system.

MINISTRIES AND STATE COMMISSIONS Ministries and state commissions are part of the State Council. They issue orders and regulations in accordance with the laws and decisions of the State Council. Some administrations

ADMINISTRATIVE DIVISIONS

China is divided into 23 provinces, five autonomous regions, four municipalities, and two SARs.

Each province is divided into cities, counties, and towns. Administrative units at the lowest level are the residents' committees. They manage public welfare, settle disputes, see to public security, and ensure that state rules are implemented and observed. They also adopt, issue, and decide on plans for the economic and social welfare of their districts.

China's five autonomous regions are Guangxi, Nei Mongol (Inner Mongolia), Ningxia, Xinjiang Uygur, and Xizang (Tibet). These areas have large communities of minority nationalities. Local people's congresses and governments are set up to exercise the right of limited self-government. The four municipalities—Beijing, Shanghai, Tianjin, and Chongqing—report directly to the central government.

and bureaus with special areas of work—such as the Economic Legislation Research Center, the Nuclear Power Administration, the Foreign Exports Bureau, and the State Administration for Taxation—report directly to the State Council instead of to their respective ministries.

THE CHINESE PEOPLE'S POLITICAL CONSULTATIVE CONFERENCE (CPPCC)

The CPPCC is an advisory body that holds consultations and offers opinions on important issues in China's political system. It consists of representatives from the Communist Party, public figures, and people's organizations.

INTERNET LINKS

www.bbc.co.uk/news/world-asia-pacific-13908155

This website gives an easy-to-understand diagram explaining how China is ruled.

www.gov.cn/english/

Learn more about the structure of the Chinese government via this site.

ECONOMY

The luscious terraced green fields of canola in Guizhou.

4

AFTER THE COMMUNIST PARTY took power in 1949, the economy was collectivized. The government seized private agricultural, industrial, and commercial enterprises and placed them under collective ownership. Everyone was to contribute to and benefit from common goals.

Under this system, however, agricultural and industrial production stagnated, and economic growth slowed. In the 1980s China began reforms aimed at making it a market-socialist economy. For the first time in years, the Chinese could own small businesses. Farmers were allowed and encouraged to grow produce for their own profit and to sell it in the "free market."

Deng Xiaoping brought effective land tenure back to the household level. The Household Responsibility System allowed peasants to lease land for a fixed period from the collective, provided they delivered to the collective a minimum quota of produce, usually basic grain. They could then sell any surplus they produced, either to the state at government procurement prices or on the newly free market. They were also free to retain any profits they might earn. Within a decade, grain production had grown by roughly 30 percent, and production of cotton, sugarcane, tobacco, and fruit had doubled.

To encourage workers, a bonus system was introduced. In addition to their basic wage, workers got bonuses for productivity, punctuality, perfect attendance, and having a good work attitude. Trade links with

The People's Republic of China is the world's second-largest economy, after the United States. With an average annual growth rate of 10 percent for the past 30 years, it is also the world's fastest-growing major economy. In addition, China is the largest exporter and second-largest importer of goods in the world. China became the world's top manufacturer in 2011, surpassing the United States.

other countries were encouraged, and special economic zones (SEZs) allowed foreign investors to build factories and operate businesses.

As the reforms fueled production increases that surprised even the reformers, the scale of change grew bolder, and by the mid-1980s the party leadership had begun the more complicated and politically delicate task of transforming the country's cumbersome system of central planning and state-owned enterprise.

Workers at a clothing factory in Huaibei. Many global textile and clothing companies manufacture their products in China due to lower labor costs.

China's economy grew at an average rate of 10 percent per year during the period 1990—2004, the highest growth rate in the world. China's GDP grew 10 percent in 2003, 10.1 percent in 2004, and 10.4 percent in 2005 despite attempts by the government to cool the economy. China's total trade in 2010 surpassed $2.97 trillion, making China the world's second-largest trading nation, after the United States. Such high growth is necessary if China is to generate the 15 million jobs needed annually to employ new entrants into the national job market.

By 2010 it was evident to outside observers such as *The New York Times* that China was poised to move from export dependency to development of an internal market. Wages were rapidly rising in all areas of the country, and Chinese leaders were calling for an increased standard of living.

In 2010 China's GDP was valued at $5.87 trillion, surpassing Japan's $5.47 trillion, and it became the world's second-largest economy, after the United States. China could become the world's largest economy (by nominal GDP) as early as 2020. China is the largest creditor nation in the world and owns approximately 24.3 percent of all foreign-owned U.S. Treasury securities.

China is also trying to promote innovation and to move from "made in China" to "innovated in China." With China's cosmopolitan and highly educated diaspora, it is no surprise that as of 2010, five of the 20 most-visited websites in the world are indexed in Mandarin. They include PRC-born behemoths such as Baidu.com, Taobao.com, and Sina.com.cn and video-sharing site Tudou.com, which has gained users in both North America and Europe.

China also launched its first manned space flight on October 15, 2003, sending astronaut Yang Liwei into space for 21 hours. The Chinese space program's long-term goal is lunar exploration.

INFLATION

Inflation is a serious challenge in China. In August 2011 it was reported as 6.5 percent, but food prices had risen by 14.8 percent during the previous year. The price of pork, China's staple meat, had increased by 57 percent from the previous year. Increased costs are systemic and not due to speculators or bad weather. The soaring cost of labor is one cause of inflation. Also, there simply is not enough low-cost, clean, and comfortable housing for ordinary citizens.

AGRICULTURE

Although China is mainly an agricultural country, only about 14.9 percent of its vast expanse of land is suitable for cultivation. Even so, China is one of the largest producers of food in the world, feeding 1.3 billion people at home and exporting rice to a number of countries, including Japan, Korea, the Philippines, Indonesia, Iraq, Russia, and Côte d'Ivoire.

Reforms in the agricultural system gave farmers incentive to produce more, and agricultural production tripled between 1978 and 1991. China is now one of the world's leading producers of grain, cotton, and rapeseed.

In the north, where the weather is cold and dry, wheat, millet, and sorghum are grown. Wheat is made into bread and noodles, whereas sorghum is used as an alternative to rice or as fodder and may be made into wine.

Rice is the most important crop in the south. It is grown mainly in the Yangtze River Valley and on the Yunnan-Guizhou Plateau. About half of the cultivated land in China is used for growing rice, and crops are harvested twice a year.

Chinese farmers planting rice seedlings.

Corn and soybeans are major crops in both the north and the south. Protein-rich soybeans are an important part of the Chinese diet.

On the flat grasslands of Mongolia, sheep and goats are raised. China now produces enough lamb for its own consumption and for export. Dairy products come from cows raised on the outskirts of large cities.

China is the world's largest producer and consumer of agricultural products, and some 300 million Chinese farmworkers are in the industry, mostly laboring on pieces of land about the size of U.S. farms. Virtually all arable land is used for food crops. China is the largest producer of rice in the world, contributing 32.7 percent of global rice production. Moreover, it is among the principal sources of wheat, corn, tobacco, soybeans, potatoes, sorghum, peanuts, tea, millet, barley, oilseed, pork, and fish. Major nonfood crops, including cotton, other fibers, and oilseeds, furnish China with a small proportion of its foreign trade revenue. Agricultural exports, such as vegetables and fruits, fish and shellfish, grain, and meat products, are sent to Hong Kong. China hopes to further increase agricultural production through improved plant stocks, fertilizers, and technology. Today agriculture contributes only 10.2 percent of China's GDP, but it employs about 38.1 percent of the labor force.

CELL PHONE AND INTERNET USAGE

The number of Internet users in China stood at 579 million by the end of 2009, or 44.5 percent of the population. China adds 31.95 million Internet users annually. Of all its netizens, 346 million used broadband, and 233 million used cell phones. China invested ¥4.3 trillion ($676 billion) from 1997 to 2009 to build a nationwide optical communication network covering 5.1 million miles (8.2 million km). China now is the country with the most Internet users in the world. China is also the country with the highest cell-phone usage in the world, with 906.8 million people carrying mobile phones.

LUXURY GOODS

The market for luxury goods in the People's Republic of China is very substantial and accounts for a significant proportion of all luxury-goods sales worldwide. As of 2010, China was the world's second-largest consumer market for luxury goods, next only to Japan and having surpassed the United States in 2009. China is the largest consumer of automobiles in the world after the United States.

Chinese luxury-goods consumers are younger than their European counterparts, belonging to the 18 to 50 age group, compared with the over-40 age group in Europe. For this reason, China's luxury-goods market is expected to grow faster than that of Europe. According to the consulting firm McKinsey & Company, 80 percent of Chinese luxury-goods buyers are under 45, compared with 30 percent of luxury-goods buyers in the United States and 19 percent in Japan. Many of the young luxury-goods buyers are self-employed or professionals. According to a report by the World Luxury Association, Chinese consumers spend a larger proportion of their income on luxury goods compared with the world average of 4 percent. Most Chinese buy luxury goods as a status symbol.

INDUSTRY

China manufactures heavy industrial goods, such as cars, trucks, planes, trains, and ships, and finished products such as electrical appliances and other consumer goods. China's most important industries include oil, iron and steel, coal, energy, machinery, electronics, and textiles.

The industrial sector grew slowly after the 1979 economic reforms due to the emphasis on agriculture and light industry. This changed in the 1990s. With increasing emphasis on industry, by 2000 industrial production had grown by 9.9 percent, mainly due to foreign investment. There are now many

Stephan Winkelmann, CEO of luxury car manufacturer Lamborghini, says, "China's super-car market is growing faster than our expectations, while the Western markets are declining. The strong demand will soon make China our second-biggest market, after the United States. If the high taxes on luxury cars are removed, China could very well become the biggest market."

foreign company enterprises in textiles and garments, electronics, chemicals, energy, transportation, and construction. Since 1979, China has approved an estimated 360,000 foreign-funded enterprises, with an investment value of $348 billion.

While most industries are scattered along the coast, industrial areas are being developed throughout the country. Guangdong Province in the south has the strongest industrial growth, as investors from neighboring Hong Kong have set up factories and businesses.

A significant development in China was the establishment of two stock exchanges, in Shanghai and Shenzhen, in 1991. Both local Chinese and foreigners are allowed to trade stocks.

Between 1978 and 2010, China's per capita GDP had grown from $153 to $7,519, while its current account surplus had increased by more than 53 times between 1982 and 2010, from $5.7 billion to $306.2 billion. During this time, China also became an industrial powerhouse, moving beyond initial successes in low-wage sectors such as clothing and footwear to the increasingly sophisticated production of computers, pharmaceuticals, and automobiles.

Machinery used in the manufacturing of cars.

SPECIAL ECONOMIC ZONES

As part of its economic reforms and policy of opening to the world, between 1980 and 1984 China established SEZs in Shantou, Shenzhen, and Zhuhai in Guangdong Province and Xiamen in Fujian Province; it also designated the entire island province of Hainan an SEZ.

Since then, 15 free-trade zones, 32 state-level economic and technological development zones, and 53 new and high-tech industrial development zones have been established in large and midsize cities.

The economic characteristics of SEZs are:

- *Construction relies primarily on attracting and using foreign capital.*
- *Most enterprises are Sino-foreign joint ventures and partnerships as well as wholly foreign-owned enterprises.*
- *Products are primarily export-oriented.*
- *Economic activities are driven primarily by market forces.*
- *SEZs are listed separately in national planning (including financial planning) and have province-level authority on economic administration. The local congress and government of the SEZs have legislation authority.*

INTERNET LINKS

http://encyclopedia.kids.net.au/page/ec/Economy_of_the_People%27s_Republic_of_China

This web page provides a wonderful overview of the economy of China.

https://www.cia.gov/library/publications/the-world-factbook/geos/ch.html

This website offers a brief summary of the rise of China's economy.

www.chinatoday.com/china.topics/china_economy.htm

This site offers a myriad of interesting articles about China's economy.

ENVIRONMENT

The beautiful waters of the Five Color Lake in Jiuzhaigou National Park.

5

CHASING THE POLITICAL GAINS of economic development, local officials in China often overlook environmental pollution, worker safety, and public-health problems. China's rapid economic growth of the past 30 years has been accompanied by severe deterioration of the environment.

Air- and water-pollution levels are among the highest in the world. Pollution has made cancer the leading cause of death in 30 cities and 78 counties. Many waterways in the country are contaminated by industrial waste, making them unfit for human use.

Nevertheless, efforts by the Chinese government since 1990 have slowed down deterioration of the environment. The government has made environmental protection a high priority. It has implemented programs and projects at the national and local levels and introduced economic reform policies on industry with stricter regulations in polluted areas.

Conservation efforts include energy and nature conservation; the switch to natural-gas use; river-basin management; reforestation; controlling industrial water and air pollution as well as vehicle emissions particularly in urban areas; and recycling. China is one of a few countries in the world that has been rapidly increasing its forest cover. It is managing to reduce air and water pollution.

In addition, there has been much growth in the domestic environmental protection industry in recent years. As part of November

2008's $498 billion economic stimulus package, the largest in China's history, the government plans to enhance sewage- and rubbish-treatment facilities and prevent water pollution; accelerate green-belt and natural-forest planting programs; and increase energy-conservation initiatives and pollution-control projects. With $34.6 billion invested in clean technology in 2009, China is the world's leading investor in renewable-energy technologies. China produces more wind turbines and solar panels each year than any other country.

CLEAN BEIJING

In a showcase effort, the government cleaned up the capital city, Beijing, for the 2008 Olympic Games big-time.

Planting and reforestation programs added greenery in the urban districts and vegetation in the mountainous areas. Households and businesses were urged to recycle waste, conserve energy and natural resources, and use public transportation. To improve air quality, the city placed restrictions on construction sites, gas stations, and the use of commercial and passenger vehicles in Beijing. From June 20 through September 20, passenger vehicle restrictions were placed on alternate days depending on the last digit of the car's license plate. It was anticipated that this measure would take 45 percent of Beijing's 3.3 million cars off the streets. It was an extremely effective though punitive measure, and Beijing's cleanliness received rave reviews during the Olympics.

AIR POLLUTION

Rapid industrialization has brought new wealth to China. Unfortunately it has also led to increased industrial effluents. Many industrialized cities live under a layer of smog. In 2008 China overtook the United States as the biggest emitter of carbon dioxide in the world. China puts out 6.2 trillion tons (5,625 million metric tons) of carbon dioxide annually, in comparison with America's 5.8 trillion tons (5,262 million metric tons). China emits close to 21 percent of the world's greenhouse gases, and the United States emits 29 percent.

The industrial sector is the biggest source of carbon emissions because coal is still the major source of energy for businesses and homes. Although it is the cheapest source of energy, coal is also the dirtiest. Coal burning in China releases 650 million tons (589.7 million metric tons) of carbon annually into the atmosphere.

WATER POLLUTION

Dumping industrial waste into waterways threatens the country's supply of drinking water. With the

China is currently the world's top emitter of carbon dioxide.

economy growing fast, controlling pollution will be difficult. About one-third of the industrial wastewater and more than 90 percent of household sewage in China is released into rivers and lakes without being treated. Nearly 80 percent of China's cities (278 of them) have no sewage-treatment facilities, and few have plans to build any. Underground water supplies in 90 percent of the cities are contaminated.

A study by China's Environmental Protection Agency in February 2010 said that water-pollution levels were double what the government had predicted them to be mainly because agricultural waste was ignored. China's first pollution census in 2010 revealed farm fertilizer was a bigger source of water contamination than factory effluent.

Water pollution—caused primarily by industrial waste, chemical fertilizers, and raw sewage—accounts for half of the $69 billion that the Chinese economy loses to pollution every year. About 11.7 million pounds (5.31 million kg) of organic pollutants are emitted into Chinese waters very day, compared with 5.5 million pounds (2.49 million kg) in the United States.

CLIMATE CHANGE IN CHINA

China's first National Assessment of Global Climate Change, released recently by the Ministry of Science and Technology, states that China already suffers from the environmental impacts of climate change: increase of surface and

A grid of straw set in Tengger Desert in a bid to slow down desertification.

ocean temperatures and rise of sea levels. Rising sea levels are an alarming trend because China has a very long and densely populated coastline, with some of the most economically developed cities, such as Shanghai, Tianjin, and Guangzhou, situated there. Chinese research has estimated that a 3.3-feet (1-m) rise in sea level would inundate 35,521 square miles (92,000 square km) of China's coast, thereby displacing 67 million people. There has also been an increased occurrence of climate-related disasters such as drought and flood, and the magnitude of the disasters is growing.

Desertification remains a serious problem, consuming an area greater than that taken by farmlands. Although desertification has been curbed in some areas, it still is expanding at a rate of more than 25.9 square miles (67 square km) every year. The decline in the rate of desertification is admirable, but it could still be reduced. A total of 90 percent of China's desertification occurs in the west of the country.

POLLUTION REDUCTION

To reduce pollution, new manufacturing plants must follow stricter emission standards. Factories in major Chinese cities such as Shanghai and Guangzhou have moved from city centers to industrial areas on the outskirts. At the same time, old plants are required to upgrade their existing facilities to become environmentally friendly. Industries are also encouraged to develop other energy sources such as wind, geothermal, hydroelectric, and solar power.

NATURE CONSERVATION

In a country as vast as China, there are hundreds of thousands of species of wildlife, some facing extinction. The most famous is the giant panda. Only about 1,000 of these endangered mammals are left, mainly in northern and northwestern Sichuan. The government launched a campaign in 1992 to protect these animals and their habitats from human encroachment and rampant logging. Other endangered animals in China include the golden monkey, the black gibbon, the Tibetan antelope, the Siberian tiger, the South China tiger, and the Bactrian camel.

The southwestern provinces have some of the country's richest and most diverse vegetation. The region has 1,227 nature reserves covering 12 percent of China's land area. To reduce the threat of erosion and flooding along major rivers, China's National Logging Ban was issued in 1998. This has increased reforestation efforts.

Previously many local governments took fertile agricultural land out of production in exchange for investments and economic growth. Stricter controls exist now to prevent that from happening again.

Although China's forest cover is only 20 percent, the country has some of the largest expanses of forested land in the world, making it a top target for forest-preservation efforts. A total of 12 percent of China's land area, or more than 274 million acres (111 million ha), is closed forest. However, UNEP also estimates that 36 percent of China's closed forests are facing pressure from high-population densities, making preservation efforts that much more crucial.

According to the Chinese government's website, the central government invested more than ¥40 billion ($6.29 billion) between 1998 and 2001 on protection of vegetation, farm subsidies, and conversion of farm to forests. Between 1999 and 2002, China converted 19 million acres (7.7 million ha) of farmland into forest.

WASTE MANAGEMENT AND RECYCLING

China creates at least 600 million tons (544.3 million metric tons) of waste each year, and much of it is not properly treated. Of this, 155 million tons (140.6 million metric tons) come from urban areas. To better manage waste and pollution, more money is needed, and sound policies need to be implemented.

The Chinese government has received international praise for its efforts to manage waste and remedy ecological damage. It is also working to include sound environmental-protection policies within the overall development strategy for the country.

INITIATIVES AND GOALS

China's Law on Environmental Protection was drafted in 1979 and passed by the NPC in 1983. It made protecting the environment a basic national policy. Since then, the government has introduced additional measures to tackle environmental problems, which have become more complicated due to increased industrial development.

Businesses are urged to use environmentally friendly building materials manufactured with energy-saving technology. One of the biggest projects ever launched is the 14-year (2001—15) cleanup of the Bohai Sea.

China has enlisted the help of international organizations, such as the International Union for Conservation of Nature and Natural Resources (IUCNNR), the World Bank, and the United Nations, on projects within its environmental-protection programs, such as grassland reclamation in Inner Mongolia and protection of Tibetan antelopes.

PLASTIC-BAG REDUCTION

As of June 1, 2008, all supermarkets, department stores, and shops have been prohibited from giving out free plastic bags. Stores must clearly mark

A man collecting garbage. China's large population has made safe and proper waste management a challenge for the government.

the price of plastic shopping bags and are banned from adding that price onto the price of products. The production, sale, and use of ultrathin plastic bags—those less than 0.00098 inches (0.02 mm) thick—are also banned. The State Council calls for "a return to cloth bags and shopping baskets." This ban, however, does not include the widespread use of cardboard shopping bags at clothing stores or the use of plastic bags at restaurants for takeout food. Since the ban, there has been a 10 percent decrease in the number of plastic bags thrown away.

In 2000 China banned plastic-foam dishware, 10 billion units of which once rolled off 130 production lines across the nation annually. The ban is part of China's commitment to phasing out ozone-depleting substances under various international agreements it has signed since the late 1980s. The government has formed an ozone-layer protection group to identify projects that can be phased out to reduce the emissions that destroy the ozone layer.

ELECTRONIC WASTE

China, where sales of electronic devices are surging, generates as much as 2.3 million tons (2.09 million metric tons) of electronic waste domestically each year, according to a report in 2010 by UNEP. That is second only to the United States. Despite improvements to treatment facilities in recent years, China still lacks large numbers of high-tech recycling facilities and relies instead on environmentally damaging methods of disposal. Some electronics waste is burned, and large amounts of hazardous material are abandoned without treatment, according to a report by *China Environment News*.

The government has begun to tackle the issue. On January 1, 2011, the State Council issued new regulations to deal with the recovery and disposal of electronic waste. Under the new regulations the government agreed to establish a treatment fund for e-waste, which will be used to grant subsidies for the recovery and disposal of electronic products.

The Three Gorges Dam is the world's largest power station in terms of installed capacity. The dam body was completed in 2006. The cost of construction of the dam was $24 billion. The Three Gorges Dam reached its design-maximum reservoir water level of 574 feet (175 m) for the first time on October 26, 2010, and during that year its intended annual power-generation capacity of 847 million MWh (84.7 TWh) was realized.

At full power, Three Gorges reduces coal consumption by 31 million tons (28 million metric tons) per year, saving millions of pollutants from being released into the atmosphere every year. Hydropower also reduces the energy needed to mine, wash, and transport coal from northern China.

The dam increased the Yangtze's barge capacity sixfold and reduced carbon dioxide emission by 630,000 tons (571,526 metric tons) annually. From 2004 to 2007, 198 million tons (180 million metric tons) of goods passed through the ship locks. Compared with using trucks, the barges reduced carbon dioxide emission by 10 million tons (9 million metric tons) and lowered costs by 25 percent. Shipping also became safer, since the gorges were notoriously dangerous to navigate.

An important function of the dam is to control flooding, which is a major problem for the seasonal river of the Yangtze. Millions of people live downstream of the dam, with many large, important cities, such as Wuhan, Nanjing, and Shanghai, situated adjacent to the river. Plenty of farmland and China's most important industrial areas are built beside the river. The dam alleviated the impact of potentially disastrous floods in 2009 and 2010. The dam discharges its reservoir during the dry season, between December and March, every year. This increases the flow rate of the river downstream and provides freshwater for agricultural and industrial usage. It also improves shipping conditions. The water level upstream drops from 574 feet (175 m) *to 476 feet (145 m), preparing for the rainy season. The water also powers the Gezhouba Dam downstream. Since the filling of the reservoir in 2003, the Three Gorges Dam has supplied an extra 2.63 cubic miles (11 cubic km) of freshwater to downstream cities and farms during the dry season.*

China also has a huge reforestation effort in the Yangtze Basin, which accelerated after terrible floods in 1998 convinced the government that it must restore tree cover upstream of the Three Gorges Dam.

One significant drawback is that the 373-mile-long (600-km-long) reservoir flooded some 1,300 archaeological sites and altered the appearance of the Three Gorges, as the water level rose more than 590 feet (180 m). Cultural and historical relics were moved to higher ground as they were discovered, but the flooding inevitably covered undiscovered relics. Some sites could not be moved because of their location, size, or design. For example, the Shen Nong Gorge Hanging Coffins are part of the cliffs, and some of them are now submerged.

INTERNET LINKS

http://thegreenreason.com/

This website provides a fascinating documentary that showcases China's efforts to hold the first "Green Olympics."

www.ifce.org/pages/conservation.html

This is a captivating website on the Chinese conservation movement with gorgeous pictures of China's endemic wildlife.

www.nature.org/ourinitiatives/regions/asiaandthepacific/china/

This charming website has articles and lovely photos about the Nature Conservancy's projects in China.

CHINESE

A group of Long Horn Miaos, a branch of the Miao people.

MORE THAN 20 PERCENT of the world population lives in China. Population distribution in China is uneven; most people live along the fertile coastal areas, especially along the Yangtze River Delta.

Sichuan Province has the most people at 80 million, or 470 people per square mile (180 per square km); Tibet has the least at 5.4 million, or 5.23 people per square mile (2.03 per square km). The cities are crowded, although 50 percent of the population lives in the countryside—China has the largest number of farmers in the world.

HAN CHINESE

The Han, the largest ethnic group in China (1.2 billion people, or nearly 92 percent of the population) and the world, originated around the Yellow, Yangtze, and Pearl rivers.

MINORITIES

The remaining 8 percent of China's population consists of 55 other ethnic groups. Found mostly along remote border regions around India, Afghanistan, Russia, Central Asia, and Vietnam, the biggest group are the Zhuang (18 million people) and the smallest are the Hezhen, living in the far northeast, with fewer than 2,000 people.

Putonghua, or Mandarin, is the language of instruction in schools, but minorities are encouraged to teach their own languages and customs to their children.

6

Today China's population is over 1.3 billion, the largest of any country in the world. According to the 2010 census, 91.51 percent of the population was of the Han nationality, and 8.49 percent were minorities. China's population growth rate is only 0.47 percent.

MANCHU There are 10.68 million Manchu, mostly in northeastern China. They have their own script and language. As China's rulers from 1644 to 1911, they have added to the richness of Chinese culture, including books written in Mandarin.

HUI, at 10 million, are another of China's largest minorities. They are Muslims who live mainly in the northwest. Their customs are similar to those of Muslims in other countries. One outstanding Hui was the famous Ming Dynasty voyager Zheng He.

LLOBA The 2,300 Lloba live in southeastern Tibet. Largely farmers, Lloba are also skilled at crafts. Hunting is important to them, and young boys start early, joining adults in hunting trips. Staple foods include corn or millet dumplings.

KOREANS Most of the 2.5 million Koreans live in northeastern China and major cities. They have their own spoken and written language and their own newspapers. Koreans tend to be fond of music and love to sing and dance at festivals.

A Kazakh man.

KAZAKHS number 1.4 million and live mainly in Xinjiang in the northwest. They have their own script and are Muslims. Many Kazakhs live by animal husbandry, moving from place to place looking for pasture. They live in tents called yurts.

YI The 7.7 million Yi live in southwestern China, in mountain areas, mainly as farmers. They have their own script and literature. Yi women live in their parents' home after marriage until their first child is born.

ZHUANG With 18 million people, Zhuang are China's largest minority group. Most of them live in Guangxi in southwestern China. They are renowned for their singing. In the past, young people chose their mates at song festivals through songs. They are predominantly Muslims.

LI The 1.3 million Li live on Hainan Island. This southern tropical island is fertile, and the Li sometimes reap three crops of rice a year. Li are known for their knowledge of herbal medicine. Li women are skilled in weaving and embroidery. They are held in high esteem by the Beijing government because they fought against Chinese Nationalist rule during the Chinese Civil War.

MIAOS At 9 million, the Miaos are among the largest minorities in southwestern China. Miaos love to sing, and their songs may be as long as 15,000 lines. They are also skilled craftsmen, although farming is the main occupation.

A group of Tibetans.

JING The 22,517 Jing live in southwestern China's Guangxi Province. They fish and farm, the main crops being rice, sweet potatoes, peanuts, and millet. They read and write the Han script, having lived among the Han for a long time, but speak Cantonese.

TIBETANS Tibet is surrounded on three sides by the highest mountains in the world, and its remoteness and inaccessibility have added to the mystery and fascination surrounding the region. It has a population of 5.4 million. Tibetans are a religious people, and their life revolves around Lamaism, a form of Buddhism. Tibetans believe in reincarnation, and the Dalai Lama—exiled by the Chinese government—is revered as a reincarnated Buddha-to-be.

Tibetans are a hospitable people. Their main occupation is farming and raising cattle. Their diet consists mainly of the grain they grow. Their favorite drink is *tsampa* (sam-pa), which is hot tea mixed with ground barley and yak butter.

UIGHURS Most of the 9 million Uighurs live in Xinjiang Province in northwestern China. They have settled in and around the oases of the Taklimakan Desert, cultivating fruit and grain and raising sheep and horses. The Uighurs, who are Muslims, speak a language similar to Turkish and write in the Arabic script. In recent decades there has been increasing Han Chinese migration to the region, and many Uighurs complain of discrimination. Han Chinese make up roughly 40 percent of Xinjiang's population, while about 45 percent are Uighurs.

MONGOLIANS Mongolians number 5.8 million and are a nomadic people who live in the northern grasslands of Inner Mongolia. They live in yurts, which can be taken down and put up in another place.

The yurt is a tent made of animal hide, supported by strong wooden poles. The cylindrical walls are padded with thick felt to keep out the cold in winter. On the roof, skylights also act as air vents for warming fires. In summer, the base of the walls can be lifted up to let in the cool breeze.

In summer Mongolians, whose main livelihood is raising cattle and horses, move around in search of grazing pastures. Their diet consists mainly of dairy products, meat, and grain. Vegetables, especially the leafy variety, are a rarity, though they eat bean sprouts, which can be grown anywhere in any season. Meat is often air-dried, and it is common to see strips of mutton hanging in and outside a yurt. Mongolians love tea boiled with milk from their cattle. Sometimes butter-fried millet is added to it to improve the taste.

A Uighur girl strikes a pose.

Poverty, wars, and rebellions forced many Chinese to leave their country in search of a better life. Most left from provinces in southern China, such as Guangdong, Fujian, and Shanghai. Some left for countries in nearby Southeast Asia, such as Thailand, Malaysia, Singapore, and Indonesia; others went as far away as Europe, Africa, the Caribbean, South America, Australia, Canada, and the United States, where in the 19th century many settled in California to dig for gold or build railways.

Overseas Chinese, or huaqiao *(hu-ah-chi-ow), practice their own customs and traditions, some of which are not practiced by mainland Chinese. Although China is opening up, it still does not allow the free practice of certain customs and traditions.*

The huaqiao *community is large, numbering about 40 million. Many who made a better living overseas sent for their relatives. This is why we find large groups from a particular province in one area. California, for example, has a large Cantonese community, and Brazil has many Chinese from Fujian Province.*

The wish of some huaqiao *is to go back to their hometown. Many who have made good have returned to rebuild their ancestral home or make donations to build schools, hospitals, and public buildings in their villages or provinces.*

Mongolians are skilled horsemen and archers. They also enjoy wrestling, singing, and dancing. Television has entered the lives of these nomads, and in the evenings they can often be found in front of a television run by a generator outside their yurt.

There are still other minority groups in China: the Derung, Jino, Hani, Lisu, Va, Nakhi, Pumi, Blang, Nu, Lahu, Achang, and De'ang peoples live in Yunnan Province; the Buyei, Dong, Sui, and Gelao peoples live in Guizhou; the Mulao and Maonan peoples live mainly in Guangxi; the She live in Fujian and Zhejiang; Daur and Oroqen live throughout Inner Mongolia; Krygyz, Xibes, and Tatars live mainly in Xinjiang; the Bonan, Tu, Salar, and Yugur peoples live mainly in Qinghai and Gansu; and the Monba live mainly in Tibet.

POPULATION BOOM

China has always been a populous country. In an agricultural country, having more children means less work for each person. The Chinese also believe that the more sons one has, the better one will be looked after in old age. Also, the family name will be passed down to future generations.

China's one-child policy was introduced in 1978 in order to curb the population growth, and to date, coupled with economic growth and women's rights, it has been extremely successful. In the 1970s there was an average of more than five births per woman. After the introduction of the one-child policy, the fertility rate in China fell to more than three births per woman in 1980, to approximately 1.8 in 2008, and to 1.54 in 2011.

Annual population growth was 0.57 percent between 2000 and 2010, a half-percentage point lower than the 1.07 percent annual growth between 1990 and 2000. On April 20, 2011, China declared victory over rapid population growth, as the release of its decennial census signaled that the focus will turn to managing the impact of a faster-than-expected rise in the number of older people. Even with the one-child policy in place, China still has 1 million more births than deaths every five weeks.

The one-child policy was implemented by the Chinese government in an attempt to control its population growth.

EFFECTS OF ONE-CHILD POLICY

As the first generation of law-enforced only children came of age, each adult child was left having to provide support for his or her two parents and four grandparents. Called the 4-2-1 Problem, this leaves the older generations more likely to depend on retirement funds or charity for support. In response, certain provinces maintained that couples were allowed to have two children if both parents were only children themselves. As of 2009, all provinces in the nation had adopted this rule. People over the age of 60 currently make up 13.3 percent of the Chinese population, highlighting the need for a well-functioning health-care and pension system. With $3 trillion in reserves, however, the Chinese government has deep pockets for the moment.

The media refer to the indulged children in one-child families as "little emperors." Being overindulged, lacking self-discipline, and being unable to adapt to adverse circumstances are traits highly associated with Chinese singletons.

The one-child policy has also led to an uneven gender ratio, as many Chinese families prefer boys, in large part because boys continue the family name. The male-to-female ratios are high in both rural and urban areas. Many Chinese couples opt for sex-selective abortion due to the ready availability of ultrasound testing.

INTERNET LINKS

http://video.travelchinaguide.com/ethnic-minorities/
This website provides videos of ethnic minorities' dances.

www.china.org.cn/e-groups/shaoshu/
This website provides lovely pictures of ethnic minorities.

www.chinahush.com/2009/12/06/family-portraits-of-all-56-ethnic-groups-in-china/
This website provides portraits of all 56 ethnic groups by a team of 14 photographers.

A 2006 *China Daily* report stated that wealthy couples are increasingly turning to fertility medicines to have multiple births, because of the lack of penalties against couples who have more than one child in their first birth; according to the report, the number of multiple births per year in China had doubled by 2006.

Busy streets in the city of Hankou.

7

THE CHINESE ATTITUDE TOWARD life is influenced by Confucian ethics, which teach respect and love for others.

The teachings of Confucius (551 B.C.–479 B.C.) address five basic relationships in life: father to son, elder brother to younger brother, husband to wife, friend to friend, and ruler to structure.

PERSONAL RELATIONSHIPS

The Chinese make every effort not to embarrass another person, whether friend or foe. They do not openly reject a request or outwardly disagree with anything. They are brought up to mask their feelings, often by smiling or laughing. If someone responds to a request with "later" and later "forgets," it probably means that he or she cannot do the favor.

When two Chinese get to know each other, they establish *guanxi* (KWAHNG-see), or relationships. They are then obliged to exchange favors and never to reject requests but to respond with "later" or "maybe."

The Chinese are also superb hosts. Tables remain filled with food even after dinner is through. To the Chinese, empty plates mean that their guests are still hungry and they have failed as hosts.

Chinese modesty does not allow them to accept flattery; instead they give it. Compliments are often brushed aside with an embarrassed laugh and a returned compliment.

FORMS OF ADDRESS

The Chinese have a title for every member of the household. This came about because historically the Chinese family was an extended one with several generations living under one roof.

A family enjoying a meal together. Family is the center of Chinese life.

The Chinese way of asking how many brothers and sisters one has is to ask how many older or younger siblings one has. Elder brothers are called *gege* (keh-keh), whereas younger ones are *didi* (tee-tee). *Jiejie* (jee-eh-jee-eh) refers to elder sisters, whereas younger ones are called *meimei* (may-may). Different sets of names are given to each maternal and paternal grandparent and each aunt and uncle.

Outside the family, Chinese of all ages are known by their last, or given, name. Most of the time, *xiao* (see-ow), meaning "little," is used as a prefix for younger people, and *lao* (lah-ow), meaning "old," is put in front of the given name of a middle-aged person to show respect for his or her age and experience. These prefixes are used only for persons one is familiar with. When formally addressing a man, the given name is put before *xian sheng* (si-anh shehng), or "Mr." Women keep their maiden names after marriage, replacing "Miss" with "Madam" after their given names.

Teachers are well respected; *laoshi* (LAH-OW-sheh), meaning "teacher," is always added after their given name. People in the streets address strangers as *tongzhi* (TONG-sheh), or "comrade," when asking for directions or buying things.

THE EXTENDED FAMILY

In China life revolves around the family. In the city it is common to find three generations living together under one roof, and in the countryside the family can extend to include uncles, aunts, cousins, and in-laws.

The oldest relative in the family is respected as a person of wisdom whose word is usually law. The elderly are well looked after even if they become bedridden. They are sent to hospitals or institutions only if the family cannot provide them with the proper care.

The greatest joy for the older generation is to see the whole family around them—the more males the better, as they are then assured that the family name will be carried on. The family hierarchy is carefully preserved, and each member of the family knows where he or she stands, even if the difference in age is only a few days. The younger generation is expected to not talk back or disobey orders from their elders.

Babies are well loved in any Chinese family. With the one-child policy in China, the child is doted on and given almost everything he or she wants. In the extended family, the baby is certainly king (or queen).

Chinese women live with their parents until they marry. Once married, a woman stays with her husband in his home. The husband continues to live with his parents, as it is his duty to look after them until their death. However, more couples are choosing to move out on their own.

With the one-child policy in effect, children are doted on more than ever in China.

GOING TO SCHOOL

The development of primary education in so vast a country as China has been a formidable accomplishment. In contrast to the 20 percent enrollment rate before 1949, in 1985 about 96 percent of primary-school-age children were enrolled in approximately 832,300 primary schools.

Children start school at the age of six and a half. Urban children go to school five days a week. The two-semester school year consists of 9.5 months; semesters begin on September 1 and March 1, with a summer vacation in July and August and a winter vacation in January and February. There are four examinations a year.

The school day starts at 8 A.M., with four periods of 45 minutes each. There is a 10-minute break between periods and a two-hour break for

Elementary-school children in class.

lunch. Afternoons are devoted to more lessons, homework, extracurricular activities, and doing chores around the school premises. The day ends at about 4:20 P.M. Urban primary schools typically divide the school week into 24 to 27 classes of 45 minutes each. In the rural areas, however, the norm is half-day schooling, more-flexible schedules, and itinerant teachers traveling from school to school. A foreign language, often English, is introduced in about the third grade.

After six years of elementary school, children go to high school. Among some of the subjects taught in high school are mathematics, a foreign language, politics, history, geography, sciences, music, and art. In the countryside, agricultural high schools can be found, where students are taught agricultural science and technology.

High school is divided into three years of junior high and three years of senior high education. Students can choose to pursue vocational training after junior high school. This prepares them for specialized jobs. Students who finish senior high school can take entrance examinations to universities or institutes that specialize in languages, research, teaching, or physical training. The National Higher Education Entrance Examination, commonly known as *gao kao* (gow kow), is held annually. This academic examination is a prerequisite for entrance into almost all universities.

MARRIAGE

Traditionally marriages were elaborate events with days of feasting and complicated rites. The wedding day would often be the first time the bride and the groom actually set eyes on each other, as marriages were prearranged by the parents.

Women have been a major labor presence in China since the People's Republic was established. Some 40 to 45 percent of all women over 15 years of age are employed.

The women of ancient China were essentially homebound and their social behavior highly controlled. Upper-class girls had their feet bound when they were between four and eight years old to stop their feet from growing. This painful process, which was considered a beauty treatment, left them with small misshapen, clublike feet as they grew older. With only tiny feet supporting their weight, they could just manage several small steps at a time. Still, their gait, like "a swaying willow tree," was considered attractive and kept them from venturing too far from home. The practice continued until well into the 20th century.

After China became a republic, the status of Chinese women was officially equal to that of men. Since 1949, the government of the People's Republic of China has actively promoted the social, economic, and political roles of women in society. These efforts met with some resistance in a traditionally Neo-Confucian society of male superiority. Nonetheless, women played a big part in rebuilding China. Most took on jobs once held only by men, such as doctors, engineers, factory workers, soldiers, and even those involving manual labor, such as farmers and porters.

Women are now an important part of the workforce. They have equal pay to men and carry the same workload. At the same time, many Chinese men share responsibilities for their children and do household chores such as cooking, cleaning, and ironing.

Women are well represented in the government and hold key positions in large organizations. It is felt that if anyone can do a job, that person should be given the responsibility, regardless of gender.

Nowadays couples can choose their partners and register their marriage in a simple civil ceremony, after which they may arrange a celebration. Usually what is considered to be an auspicious date will be picked. A popular date is the seventh day of the seventh moon. According to an old story this is the only day that a fairy from heaven gets to meet her mortal husband. Some couples may even enlist the help of a temple fortune-teller to pick an auspicious date based on their birth dates and times.

A couple taking wedding pictures in the garden in Moller Villa in Shanghai.

After the date is selected, wedding details such as types and quantities of betrothal gifts, reciprocal gifts, the bride's price, and the number of tables at the wedding banquet provided by the groom's parents for the bride's parents' guests are settled.

Fall months are popular for weddings, as the weather is good and the moon is at its brightest. In the country, the winter months are also good for weddings, as work on the farm is relatively slow, and time can be spent cooking a feast for the whole village.

Before the wedding day, the groom's family buys electrical appliances such as a refrigerator for the couple's new home, if they can afford one, and a trousseau and jewelry for the bride.

On the wedding day, the groom makes his way to the bride's house in a limousine or bus hired for the occasion. The bride and the groom are dressed in their best clothes, though many brides now wear a white wedding gown. Chinese weddings are very lively and fun affairs where playfulness and teasing are the name of the game. In ancient times, couples were matched and wed very young, so it was necessary for the families to ease tension and anxiety by playing games with them.

After the games, the couple goes to the groom's house, where the bride will meet the rest of her new family and the celebrations continue. Wedding guests usually give the bride and groom red packets of money to defray the cost of the wedding.

CHILDBIRTH

There is often great excitement when a wife conceives. The expectant mother is well looked after and well fed. Chinese mothers usually hold full-time jobs and continue to work until the seventh month of pregnancy, when they are given lighter tasks. In cities, mothers are by law given three months of paid maternity leave.

Customs concerning childbirth are more prevalent in the countryside than in the city. Pregnant women are not allowed to join in any social occasions, especially weddings and funerals, from the start of pregnancy to 100 days after the child is born.

There are more taboos after birth, perhaps because some homes are far from medical facilities. Women are not allowed to bathe, wash their hair, or do any household chores for one month after the birth of their child. This is because the Chinese believe that the mother needs to let her body recover from the trauma of childbirth and that if she bathes, she will get severe rheumatism as she ages.

During this time, the mother regains her strength with plenty of rest and good food. Fresh, uncooked fruit and vegetables are avoided, as they are believed to be too yin, and therefore too cooling, to the system and may cause the mother to fall ill. The mother's diet consists mainly of noodles, eggs, and chicken. Fresh anchovies are often made into a soup, as this is believed to increase the production of breast milk for the newborn.

DEATH

The body is taken to the nearest crematorium, bathed, and dressed in funeral clothes. It is then placed in a glass coffin for friends and family to pay their last respects before cremation. After cremation, the ashes are placed in a special box and put in the crematorium or taken home.

A Chinese woman pays her respects to her deceased family member.

In the countryside, where burial is more common than cremation, people make their own elaborately decorated coffins. Preparations for death start when a person is still alive. Once people reach 50 years of age or so, they or their children will start making a coffin. Once it is finished, it is stored in the house until the time of death. This may sound morbid, but people are happy to know that their children will carry out the last rites.

Death rites in the countryside start with a wake that can last up to one week. Friends and relatives come from near and far to partake in a feast and pay their last respects. The family of the deceased wear white hoods and robes. Sacrificial items such as paper money, paper houses, and paper cars are burned to make sure the deceased will be comfortable in the afterlife. The coffin is then buried on the family's land.

When a death occurs in a family, all statues of deities in the house are covered up with red paper, so as not to be exposed to the body or the coffin, and all mirrors are removed, as it is believed that one who sees the reflection of a coffin in a mirror will shortly have a death in his or her family. A white cloth is hung over the doorway to the house, and a gong is placed to the left of the entrance if the deceased is a male and to the right if female.

The government is trying to discourage burial in favor of cremation.

CHINESE HOMES

Country houses are spacious. They are often part of walled compounds, with a simple wooden door opening into a courtyard. On either side of the courtyard is a kitchen and a storeroom or an extra bedroom. Facing the entrance is the main hall, consisting of the living room and one or two bedrooms. There is often a water pipe in the kitchen and another in the courtyard. Toilet facilities are found outside the house and are shared by two or three families.

In the city, similar houses are very cramped; three or four families may share a courtyard. More-fortunate urbanites live in hard-to-get apartments with a kitchen, a living room, a bedroom, and a toilet. Homes seldom have bathrooms; often the only source of water is at the kitchen sink. Shower facilities are provided by most companies on their premises for their staff. In addition, there are public baths. The multifunction living room is used to entertain guests and have meals, and at night it serves as an extra bedroom.

Every available space is used for storage. It is common to see boxes of belongings stacked on cupboards, under beds, and along corridors. Even windowsills are put to good use for storing or drying food for the winter.

As standards of living improve, and with government encouragement, it is becoming fashionable for the middle class in Shanghai, Guangzhou, and Beijing to buy homes of their own.

TRADITIONAL CHINESE DRESS

Most Chinese wear Western-style clothes. Adults own at least one Mao-style suit. Usually made of thick, dark blue cotton, it is a simple tunic with buttons down the front.

The Mao-style suit made its appearance when China became a republic; it was first used as a uniform in the army. Later it became widely worn even by civilians because its simple design and tough fabric were practical in lean times when all people wanted was something warm and durable.

Women also took to wearing Mao-style suits. Before the Cultural Revolution, women wore the cheongsam, a long slim dress with a modest slit up the side, to formal functions. This feminine dress was later discouraged, but it has since made a comeback among women in the cities.

TRADITIONAL CHINESE MEDICINE

Traditional Chinese medicine has its origins in the countryside, where people discovered by trial and error that combinations of certain herbs relieved certain ailments. Books listing herbs and their functions were written as far back as the Han Dynasty.

A Chinese pharmacy stocks and dispenses traditional medicine. Rows and rows of wooden drawers cover the walls in the pharmacy, each containing a kind of herb. Prescriptions are made up by combining several kinds of herbs. There is usually a doctor of Chinese medicine in attendance. By taking the patient's pulse, looking at the color of the tongue and the skin, and noting other symptoms, the doctor can diagnose the problem. A simple headache can be linked to organs such as the liver or the kidney that are temporarily under stress and not functioning well. Medicine is prescribed to relieve the headache and a tonic recommended to get the organ back to normal. As herbs are slow-acting, they have to be taken over a long period of time.

Traditional Chinese medicine is taken not just to relieve a symptom or cure an illness but also to improve bodily functions. Brews of herbs, leaves, barks, and berries are cooked for hours before being consumed. Sometimes more-exotic ingredients such as animal horns, dried snakes and lizards, and the fat glands of the Manchurian snow frog are added for a more potent brew.

Besides herbal medicine, traditional medical treatment includes massage, deep-breathing exercises, and acupuncture.

ACUPUNCTURE Acupuncture is based on the Chinese theory that the body has a network of energy lines known as meridians. These meridians are linked, and they affect the major organs of the body. According to the theory, when a person is not feeling well, it is thought that there is an imbalance of yin and yang or an uneven distribution of chi, a vital energy or life force.

Along the meridians are certain points where needles are placed to get the chi to flow again. Different-size needles are used to pierce the skin at varying angles and depths. They are then twirled or vibrated by hand or electronically until a numbing sensation is felt.

There are more than 300 acupuncture points throughout the body. In the course of treating an ailment, it is common practice to stick needles in the ears, on the face and the neck, and in between the fingers and the toes. Like traditional Chinese herbal medicine, acupuncture should be carried out over a period of time to be fully effective.

Acupuncture is commonly used as an anesthetic in China and in other countries. With acupuncture, even major surgery can be performed with the patient fully conscious and feeling no pain at all. It is even used for weight loss and dieting.

INTERNET LINKS

www.chinesefortunecalendar.com/yinyang.htm
This website furnishes an interesting account on the origin of the yin-yang symbol.

www.chineseknotweddings.com/traditional/chinese-wedding-games
This website provides an informal guide to traditional Chinese wedding games.

www.topchinatravel.com/china-guide/traditional-chinese-clothing/
This website provides everything one might want to know about Chinese clothing.

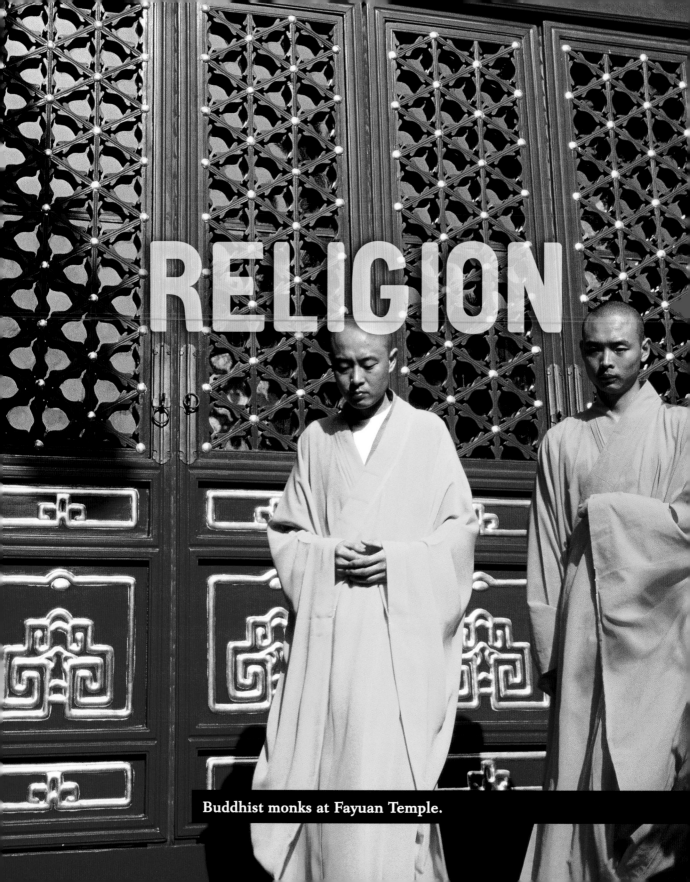

RELIGION

Buddhist monks at Fayuan Temple.

8

Generally the percentage of people who call themselves religious in China has been the lowest in the world.

TO MOST CHINESE, RELIGION is a mixture of various Chinese philosophies. Apart from the Christians and the Muslims, most Chinese practice a mixture of Taoist, Confucian, and Buddhist beliefs.

Taoism, Confucianism, and Buddhism began as philosophies. Their teachings relate to living in harmony with nature. They later became popular religions and were intermingled by the Chinese so that, for example, a Taoist could have Confucian and Buddhist beliefs as well.

Chinese are generally superstitious, the result of the Taoist belief of keeping in harmony with nature and the universe. To ensure good luck in major events such as marriage or moving to new premises, people appeal to the gods' goodwill by choosing an auspicious date and time on the lunar calendar, when the moon is full or when zodiac signs do not clash. Firecrackers are set off to scare away offending spirits, and red is used almost everywhere to attract good fortune.

The Chinese authorities, however, disapprove of too much superstition, believing that it inhibits one's thinking and actions. The younger generation is less superstitious than those born in pre-communist times (before 1949).

Although the constitution of 1982 guarantees religious freedom, the majority of Chinese are atheists, as most grew up during the Cultural Revolution when religious groups were persecuted.

The government of the People's Republic of China is officially atheist, having viewed religion as emblematic of feudalism and foreign colonialism, and it maintains separation of the state and the church. This is a change from the Cultural Revolution, which encouraged the elimination of religions and led to the destruction of a massive number of places of worship. This policy relaxed considerably in the late 1970s at the end of the Cultural Revolution, and more tolerance of religious expression has been permitted since the 1980s.

TAOISM

Taoism teaches humans to live in harmony with nature. Taoists believe in supernatural beings, use charms and spells, meditate, and keep to a vegetarian diet. They believe that these practices can help them gain immortality and be one with the universe. Taoism was founded by the philosopher Laozi, whose name means "Old Master."

CONFUCIANISM

Born in 551 B.C., Confucius was a government official who became a teacher of moral philosophy later in life. His philosophy became the backbone of Chinese thinking and behavior.

Confucius lived in a time of political violence and social disorder. He devoted his life to the teaching of *ren* (rehn), or the love of humankind. Linked to this is *xiao* (si-ow), or filial piety, devotion to one's parents. Ancestor worship ensures that this devotion continues after the death of the parents. Tablets bearing the name of the deceased are kept in homes, and the deceased are honored and remembered, especially on their birthdays and death anniversaries.

Other qualities connected with *ren* are loyalty, courage, wisdom, and trustworthiness. The aim of cultivating such qualities is to become a superior person. Confucianism also encourages interest in the arts to stimulate the mind. Confucianism has been experiencing a great revival in China in the 21st century, as it is supported by the central government.

A Taoist priest at the Dongyue Temple in Beijing.

BUDDHISM

Buddhism was brought to China along the Silk Road by Indian merchants. By the sixth century A.D. it was a major religion in China. Chinese monks journeyed to India and Sri Lanka to bring back Sanskrit scriptures and sutras to be translated into Chinese. The recorded journeys of traveling monks have become important historical literature. In China the Buddhist philosophy absorbed Taoist and Confucian ideas. In Tibet, Buddhism blended with Bön, an indigenous ancient religion of Tibet, to become Lamaism.

ISLAM

Islam came into China via Arab and Persian merchants around the seventh century. Scholars and missionaries arrived, and mosques were built. The integration of Islam with Chinese society is seen in the way Muslims changed their names to Chinese family names: Muhammad, Mustafa, and Masoud have become Mo, Mai, and Mu.

Worshipers at their prayers at the Great Mosque in Xining.

Feng shui, which literally means "wind and water," is the practice of living in harmony with the natural environment for good fortune and health. It was first practiced in ancient China by farmers, to whom wind and water were very important natural forces that could either destroy or nurture their crops.

Today feng shui has developed into the art of placing and creating buildings and other man-made structures such as fountains and bridges so that they harmonize with and benefit from the surrounding physical environment.

The Chinese believe that there are invisible forces beneath the earth— positive yang and negative yin. A compass called a luopan *(lu-ow-pahn) measures these forces. Balancing the two forces in a person's immediate surroundings is important for good health and fortune. For example, warm colors representing the positive force in a room should be balanced by cool colors representing the negative force.*

A building should ideally be situated with a hill protecting the back and calm water in front for a soothing view. A huge tree that shadows the main entrance could prevent fortune from entering, while a swift flowing drain or river nearby could carry all the luck away. Doors are sometimes built at an angle to prevent bad luck from entering, and mirrors are hung above doors or windows to scare away evil spirits with their own reflections.

CHRISTIANITY

The earliest Christians to arrive in China, in A.D. 735, were Nestorian Christians from Syria. In the 16th century, the Jesuits came, bringing with them scientific knowledge. When China opened up to the world after the Opium Wars, Protestant and Roman Catholic missionaries arrived. Although Christian missionaries opened schools, universities, and hospitals, Christianity never became a popular religion in China.

THE CHINESE TEMPLE

The Chinese temple is a fascinating place. Its halls are filled with statues of gods and demigods. Some of these are celestial beings, others are mythical characters, and some are individuals elevated from the status of mere mortals because of their brave or outstanding feats.

A pair of door gods, usually stone lions, guard the main entrance. They are said to have guarded a passage used by spirits a long, long time ago. Wicked spirits were weeded out by the door gods and then bound and fed to tigers. It became a tradition to paint the door gods' images on temple doors to scare away evil spirits who might want to slip in.

Inside the temple, incense and paper offerings are burned in the courtyard. Offerings of food and drink are made at the altar in the main hall. The fragrance of joss sticks, or incense, fills the air, and candles and oil lamps light the dim interior. Worshippers give thanks for wishes granted or pray for blessings for a better life.

A popular goddess is Guanyin, who can manifest herself in thousands of forms. Also known as the goddess of mercy, she is said to be sympathetic to her followers and to help them in times of trouble.

In every nook and cranny of the temple, deities representing health, wealth, and longevity and images of the Buddha are found. The most popular Buddha figure is the bald, smiling Buddha with a protruding belly, whose disposition represents wealth, joy, and long life.

INTERNET LINKS

http://fengshui.about.com/

This website provides some practical suggestions on how to apply feng shui in your life.

www.travelchinaguide.com/intro/religion/confucianism/

This website provides an illustrated account of Confucianism.

The Leshan Giant Buddha was built during the Tang Dynasty (618-907). It is carved out of a cliff face in Sichuan Province, near the city of Leshan. The stone sculpture faces Mount Emei, with the rivers flowing below its feet. It is the largest carved stone Buddha in the world. It has been listed as a UNESCO World Heritage Site and fortunately was not damaged by the 2008 Sichuan earthquake.

LANGUAGE

Bright signs light up the streets on Nathan Road in Hong Kong.

9

C HINA HAS A WEALTH OF languages. Besides Putonghua (Mandarin), the official language, eight major dialects are spoken across different regions. These dialects vary from one province to another and even from village to village.

About one-fifth of the world's population, or more than 1 billion people, speak some variety of Chinese as their native language.

MAJOR DIALECTS

The northern dialect, or Bei Fang Hua, forms the basis of Putonghua, China's official language, and is spoken by Chinese living in the northern, central, and southwestern provinces. More than 70 percent of the Chinese population speaks this dialect.

Two elderly shopkeepers enjoying a midafternoon chat.

Men from the province of Fujian engaged in a card game. One of the dialects spoken in Fujian is Hokkien.

The Wu dialect is spoken by people around Shanghai, Jiangsu, and Zhejiang provinces. Xiang is spoken in Hunan Province, the Gan dialect is spoken in Jiangxi and Hubei provinces, and Keija (Hakka) is spoken in parts of Guangdong, Fujian, and Jiangxi provinces.

The northern Min dialect is spoken in parts of Fujian and Taiwan, whereas southern Min is spoken in southern Fujian, parts of Hainan, and most of Taiwan, as well as by many overseas Chinese. Another dialect spoken by many overseas Chinese and throughout Guangdong and southeastern Guangxi provinces is Yue (Cantonese).

The written form of all Chinese dialects is the same. So while a northerner may not be able to communicate verbally in dialect with a southerner, they can read each other's writing.

PUTONGHUA

Since 1949 Putonghua, also known as Mandarin, has been taught in schools across China. The Chinese language is the oldest continuously used language in the world today. It also has more speakers than any other language in the world. Spoken Chinese has 400 sounds but 40,000—50,000 characters or words in written form. The limited number of sounds is made up for by variation in tones.

There are four tones in Putonghua to distinguish words:
- high and level (as in "high noon")
- rising (as in asking "Here?")
- falling and rising (as in asking "May I... ?")
- high and falling (as in exclaiming "No!" in an argument)

The same word said in different tones can have different meanings. For example:

Ni you bing [first tone] *ma*? (nee yo ping mah) means "Do you have some ice?"

Ni you bing [third tone] *ma*? means "Do you have a cookie?"

Ni you bing [fourth tone] *ma*? means "Are you ill?"

MINORITY LANGUAGES

The 55 minorities of China, some of which have subgroups, speak their own languages. The four main minority language groups are Altaic, Tibeto-Burmese, Tai, and Miao-Yao.

The Altaic language group includes the Turkic languages spoken by the Uighurs and Kazakhs in Xinjiang and the dialects of the Mongolians in Inner Mongolia. The Tibetans, the Yi, and the Tujia, who live mainly in the west and the southwest, speak Tibeto-Burmese languages.

Hill people in southern Sichuan and certain parts of Yunnan also speak Tibeto-Burmese languages. The Tai language group is spoken by a large number of minorities in Guangxi, Yunnan, and Guizhou. The Miao and Yao languages are closely related to each other and belong to the Sino-Tibetan family.

After 1949 institutes specializing in the research and development of minority languages were set up. One of their aims was to help minorities develop their own written script using the Latin alphabet.

Chinese is distinguished by its high level of internal diversity, although all varieties of Chinese are tonal and analytic. There are between 7 and 13 main regional groups of Chinese (depending on classification scheme), of which the most spoken, by far, is Mandarin, with about 850 million speakers.

Lessons in China are conducted in Putonghua.

Lessons for minority children are conducted in Putonghua, but the school curriculum also includes lessons in their home language. Minority languages are used locally in books, newspapers, and magazines. Radio and television programs in major minority languages such as Mongolian, Tibetan, Uighur, Kazakh, and Korean are aired daily.

THE WRITTEN LANGUAGE

There are about 50,000 characters in the Chinese script, of which only 3,000 are in common use. It is not surprising that no one knows all the characters.

Developed about 6,000 years ago, Chinese characters are among the oldest form of written languages in the world. The Chinese first started expressing their ideas in drawings. Sometimes whole pictures were drawn, and sometimes just the outline or representative part of an idea was used. These pictures and outlines are known as ideographs—for example, "sun," 日; "sheep," 羊; and "horse," 马.

In the early stages, one ideograph represented just one word. As more words were introduced, two or more ideographs were combined to form new

In 1899 a Qing Dynasty court official fell ill and sent for medicine. Bone fossils were prescribed as medication. When this was brought to him, he noticed that the bones were engraved with Chinese characters. He quickly ordered all the bones from the pharmacy to be brought to him. It was discovered that these bones, found by farmers and sold as medicine, dated as far back as the 16th century B.C. More than 1,500 words were recognized.

The bone inscriptions were vitally important in tracing the evolution of the Chinese script. They explained, for example, why the character for "sun," formerly written as a dot within a circle, evolved into a square: It was because of the shape of the bones and the simple carving tools used to inscribe words.

ideographs. For example, the ideograph for "combine," 合, and the ideograph for "hand," 手, together mean "to take," 拿. Sometimes words express whole ideas. Take *xiuxi* (si-yoo-si), meaning "rest," 休息: "man" 人 "under a tree" 木 "resting his eyes" 目 and "heart" 心.

There are 11 basic strokes, and Chinese characters are written in a proper sequence. Written out of sequence, the word often loses its form and proportion. When children first learn how to write, they practice for hours drawing dots, dashes, and strokes. They soon learn how to decipher the sequence in which to write a word they see for the first time. The simplest words have only one stroke, whereas the most complicated have 30.

The Chinese take their handwriting seriously, as it reflects their character and upbringing. Often one's handwriting is a deciding factor in whether the letter will be read or put aside for consideration. People of high standing often have very distinctive handwriting and are often privileged to put their handwriting on important signs or letterheads. There is even a restaurant in Beijing displaying an example of an emperor's handwriting because he stopped by one night and enjoyed the dumplings.

In 1964 the Chinese government introduced a form of simplified words. These have fewer strokes than the original words but keep the basic shape

A knowledge of 3,000 Chinese characters is required to read a Chinese newspaper.

An elderly woman writing Buddhist scripture with a brush.

and meaning. For example, the word "bird," originally written as 鳥, is now written as 鸟.

In an attempt to make Mandarin more intelligible to the Western world, a system known as pinyin was developed. The system phonetically translates Chinese words into romanized script.

CHINESE IDIOMS

In everyday conversation, the Chinese sprinkle their speech with idioms and puns. Using the correct idiom at the right time is appreciated as a sign of culture or wit.

Some idioms are fairly straightforward, such as *lao ma shi tu* (lah-ow mah sheh tu), meaning "an old horse knows the road." Others may not make sense unless one knows the story behind the saying. For example, *hua she tian zu* (hu-ah sheh ti-ahn zhu), meaning "to draw a snake and add feet to it," describes someone who has already completed something but spoils it by overdoing things.

The story behind the snake saying is as follows: There were some men who discovered a jar of wine that held enough only for one person to drink. They decided to hold a contest to see who could draw a snake in the sand. The fastest one got to drink the wine. The man who finished first had so much time to spare that he added feet to his snake. Then he snatched up the wine jar, claiming it was his as he had finished first. The man who finished next insisted that although his friend had indeed finished first, there was no such thing as a snake with feet, so the wine rightfully belonged to him.

Shou zhu dai tu (show zhu tie too), meaning "guarding the tree and waiting for the hare," describes one who leaves things to chance. In the story, a farmer saw a hare running so fast that it crashed into a tree and broke its neck. The farmer happily had it for dinner that night and went to the same spot the next day to wait for another hare to do the same thing.

Another saying is *ba miao zhu zhang* (pa meow zhu chang), meaning "to pull the shoots to help it to grow." It is a lesson for those who are impatient. There was a farmer who thought his rice plants were taking a long time to grow. So he pulled the new shoots upward. Then he looked at them with satisfaction for the shoots were indeed taller. He went home to tell his family what he had done. Later when his family went to see, they found a field of dead plants.

INTERNET LINKS

www.chinese-tools.com/chinese/proverbs/01.html

This website provides an account of enchanting Chinese proverbs and their meanings.

www.chineselanguage.com

This is an instructional website on the Chinese language, with audio files on pronunciation.

www.instructables.com/id/HOW-TO-COUNT-TO-TEN-ON-ONE-HAND-in-Chinese/

This website provides a pictorial guide of how the Chinese count to 10 on one hand.

ARTS

An ethnic Bai woman embroidering.

10

MANY STYLES OF ART in China developed during the Tang Dynasty, when artistic expression reached a sophisticated level.

DECORATIVE ART

Chinese decorative art captures symbols of nature and myth on fabric, porcelain, ceramics, and other materials.

Around the seventh century, a white clay was discovered along the banks of the Yellow and Yangtze rivers. This clay produced white porcelain pieces that craftsmen were able to refine so that they were eggshell thin and translucent. Perhaps the most popular of these are the blue-and-white Ming porcelain pieces. They became so famous in the West that they were called "china," after their place of origin.

A woman filling color into a cloisonné art piece. Cloisonné is a technique brought to China from Persia.

The market for Chinese art, both antique and contemporary, is widely reported to be among the hottest and fastest-growing in the world, attracting buyers all over the world. The Voice of America reported in 2006 that modern Chinese art was raking in record prices both internationally and in domestic markets, with some experts fearing the market might be overheating.

Another colorful art form is cloisonné. Enamel paint, blue being the most popular, is used to fill in thin plates that are then soldered onto metal bases. A skill brought to China from Persia during the Ming Dynasty, cloisonné decorates everything from grandfather clocks to chopsticks.

The Chinese also refined the art of carving. They usually carve jade or ivory, using special knives as small as toothpicks to create the fine details.

OPERA

This classic form of entertainment started out as street performances where gongs, cymbals, and drums were used to attract the audience. This "cacophony" is still the trademark of Chinese opera and marks the start of each new scene.

Each region has its own style of opera. Some stress singing, others acrobatics or dancing. Sung in the local dialects, operas are still performed as outdoor entertainment.

The most popular style of Chinese opera comes from Beijing; it originated 200 years ago. It took the best aspects of the different styles from other

A colorful Beijing opera performance.

THE MONKEY KING

The Monkey King, or Sun Wukong, is probably the best-loved character in Chinese opera. There are between 500 and 600 operas that revolve around his adventures and antics. Most of these stories are based on the novel Journey to the West *written by Wu Cheng'en in the 16th century.*

Sun Wukong, a celestial being, accompanies his master, a Buddhist monk, to India in search of religious scriptures. Along the way he endures all kinds of dangers and hardships and protects his master from demons and evil beings.

Totally devoted to his master, he is a clever, cunning, and disobedient character with a good heart. His monkeylike antics and mischief amuse audiences of all ages.

Most operas about Sun Wukong are filled with acrobatics. Somersaults, tumbles, and falls make up most of the spectacular fighting scenes. Actors who play the Monkey King spend their whole careers perfecting the art and are able to imitate the actions and characteristics of the monkey.

parts of China and integrated them into a style that includes singing, dancing, mime, and acrobatics.

The operas tell stories from historical epics, folk legends, classical novels, and fairy tales. Lines are sung in classical Chinese with lyrics flashed by the side of the stage so that the audience can follow the story or sing along, which they often do. Accompanying music is provided by an orchestra that includes Chinese fiddles, flutes, wooden clappers, lutes, drums, cymbals, and gongs.

An evening at the opera can be a three- or four-hour affair. Whole families turn up for performances, and the atmosphere in the theater is rowdy and almost festive, with drinks and dried melon seeds passed around. Shouts of "*Hao!*" (how), meaning "Good," punctuate solo performances and exciting combat scenes. Spectators who stand up and join in the chorus are sometimes as entertaining as the actors. Chinese love the opera, and often one finds old men walking in the streets, transistor radios held to their ears, listening intently to one.

Elaborate Chinese headdresses used by opera performers.

OPERA PARAPHERNALIA

There are four major roles in each opera. The *sheng* (shehng), or male lead, is either an older man or a military or civilian hero, who is almost always strong, handsome, and intelligent. *Dan* (dun) characters are female leads who are dignified virtuous women, younger women who are witty and charming, or military heroines. The *jing* (ching), or *dahualian* (ta-hu-ah-li-an), meaning "big painted face," is a male actor with a painted face emphasizing his strength or social standing. *Chou* (chow), or *xiaohualian* (si-ow-hu-li-an), meaning "small painted face," is the clown. He lends comic relief to the more serious scenes. These lead players are distinguished by the costumes and makeup they wear.

Heavily embroidered and in dazzling colors, opera costumes liven up a relatively bare stage. Military heroes wear padded armor and splendid headdresses with long pheasant feathers. Men and women wear fluid robes with long "water" sleeves, which they use for effect in flirting, crying, and showing fear and anger.

Stage makeup is as fascinating as the costumes. Actors paint their faces according to the roles they play. Red represents loyalty and uprightness. White is for slyness and treachery. Yellow is for craftiness or cleverness. Blue and green represent evil spirits, whereas silver and gold color the faces of gods and fairies. Heroes and heroines usually have simple white- or pink-based faces with exaggerated eye makeup. Regular theatergoers are able to identify characters by their makeup.

Props may be only a table and two chairs against a painted canvas backdrop. The audience has to exercise its imagination to follow the story. One flag carried by a soldier represents a thousand men, two flags with wheels painted on them are a chariot, and a flag with appropriate characters written on it may indicate a flood or strong winds. Actors who jump off chairs are trying to drown themselves in rivers or wells, while those climbing tables and chairs are crossing hills and mountain ranges.

ACROBATICS

This performing art is 22 centuries old in China. It started out as a means of livelihood for farmers during the winter months and developed into one of the most popular forms of entertainment in China and abroad.

Props used are often household items such as dishes and furniture. These objects are often tossed in the air or piled precariously one on top of another. Balancing acts on bicycles, piles of chairs, or large urns are common, and so are contortionist acts. Acrobatic acts often include performing animals.

Acrobats are so popular that there are acrobatic troupes that represent towns and large associations. There are currently more than 120 acrobatic troupes at county level and above, involving more than 12,000 performers.

In the past 40 years many Chinese acrobatic troupes have toured more than 100 countries to promote friendship and cultural exchanges.

Training for the opera is rigorous, and actors start when they are as young as 10 years old.

CALLIGRAPHY

Chinese calligraphy is more than handwriting—it is an art. A well-written piece conjures up images of strength, beauty, or grace. Characters can look graceful and feminine or strong and masculine, even vigorous, forceful, hot, or cold. Calligraphers write poems, couplets, or proverbs to be hung on the walls.

The Chinese place great importance on good calligraphy, and from the Tang to the Qing dynasties a scholar's handwriting carried great weight in his score on the civil service examination. Poets take as much pride in the writing as in the content of their poems.

There are several forms of calligraphy. One is a formal style with regular characters that are angular, with no circles and few curved lines. Then there is the *cao shu* (chao shu), or grass style, thus named because writing in this style appears as if the wind has blown over the grass. Only those who have studied calligraphy for a long time can decipher words written in this style. Another style is the *kai shu* (khai shu), developed 2,000 years ago but still used by the Chinese today as regular writing.

The tools for Chinese calligraphy are few—brush, ink stick, inkstone, and paper (sometimes silk). These are known as the four treasures of calligraphy.

PAINTING

Chinese painting involves five subjects: human figures, landscapes, flowers, birds and land animals, and fish and insects. Paintings are usually done on silk or absorbent paper made of bamboo pulp. A pointed brush is used to apply paint made of mineral and plant pigments. Color, if used at all, is applied in small amounts for a washed look.

Chinese paintings strive to catch the spirit of the subject. Artists sometimes meditate before picking up the brush and in a burst of energy put an image to paper. Works are painted from memory and executed quickly and confidently. Unlike Western art, a picture is completed within minutes, and an artist may paint the same subject again and again until the desired effect is achieved. Many famous artists specialize in painting just one subject, such as birds, insects, shrimp, or even donkeys.

The types of brushstrokes are important, as they contribute to the texture of the painting. They are given fancy names such as "rain drops," "ax cuts," or "wrinkles on a devil's face." Calligraphy is almost always used to complete a Chinese painting. A couplet or a poem complements the picture.

Finger painting started in the Tang Dynasty and is regarded as a high art form. The fingernails are the main tools. They are kept long and well shaped, as a broken nail hinders the artist.

MUSICAL INSTRUMENTS

When Emperor Qin Shi Huang ordered all books to be burned, most musical instruments were destroyed as well. What we see today are mostly tribal instruments that were adapted or adopted by the Han to make music. Below are some instruments found in a Chinese orchestra.

ERHU (erh-who) A fiddle with two strings played with a bow made of bamboo and horsehair. The *erhu* usually has a cylindrical sound box made of wood or bamboo. Animal hide such as sheepskin or snakeskin is stretched over one of its sides, creating different qualities of sound. Some of these fiddles are made of simpler materials such as coconut shells.

PIPA (pi-pah) A lute with four strings. It is held upright, and its strings can be strummed or plucked. The *pipa* is popular in the towns along the Yangtze River. Entertainers in teahouses strum their instruments while telling stories or singing.

GUZHENG (ku-zhehng) A large zither with 18 or 21 strings. It is played like a horizontal harp and sounds almost like one. In ancient times, playing the *guzheng* was considered a status symbol—to be able to play it was to be cultured.

A guzheng.

ARCHITECTURE

Chinese buildings have distinctive roofs and structures constructed from a series of vertical wooden pillars that increase gradually in height, giving them their unique shape.

Chinese buildings are built in clusters. Courtyard-style houses have buildings on each side of a square with interconnecting halls. The main house faces south so that it is warm in winter and cool in summer. In the old days, the head of the household lived here, while the servants and children lived in the side buildings.

Paper cutouts are frequently used to decorate homes for special occasions.

Temples and palaces have a similar layout. They are more elaborately built with more courtyards lying side by side or one behind the other.

One of the most charming aspects of Chinese buildings is their elaborate ornamentation. Beams are often of red lacquer with flowers painted on them. Figures of animals and people are painted on glazed tiles. Palaces are even more splendidly decorated with paintings of dragons and auspicious flowers and plants decorating ceilings, pillars, and walls. Doors of palaces are always painted red for good luck and have rows of nine gold studs running vertically and horizontally.

The Chinese believe that nine is the luckiest number: To reach 10 is to be at the end of the line, but 9 means a person is still living and achieving.

PAPER CUTOUTS

Women in the countryside may spend their free time cutting paper patterns. The patterns can be simple symmetrical patterns or complicated motifs with birds, animals, flowers, or popular opera characters. Some can even be of an entire scene from daily life.

Paper cutouts are often used to decorate the house during special occasions such as the Spring Festival. Stuck on lanterns, windows, doors, and walls, these are often designs of flowers or symbols of good luck, longevity, and health. Paper cutouts of the double happiness character are used during weddings to adorn gifts and sacrificial offerings, dowries, candlesticks, and incense burners. Paper cutouts are also used as stencils for embroidery or indigo prints that go on clothes, bed linen, or curtains.

Paper-cutting designs are often handed down from generation to generation and differ from village to village. The appeal of this art form lies in its simplicity. It can be picked up and put down at any time.

The excitement of unfolding a paper cutout lies in the fact that one never knows what to expect from a piece. Each piece is original.

EMBROIDERY

Embroidery was refined to an art form by women who wanted to wear something more than plain cloth. In the old days, a girl's embroidery skill would indicate whether she would make a good wife.

Embroidery first gained popularity with the invention of silk thread. Clothes, shoes, fans, purses, and hair accessories were decorated with embroidery. Motifs are different for men and women. Flowers, butterflies, geometric designs, and phoenixes decorate women's clothes and accessories, while dragons and bold solid designs are considered masculine.

Embroidery is also used to decorate altar cloths, flags, banners, and wall hangings. The designs are often of calligraphic characters, scenes of nature, and images of people and animals.

Elaborate pieces of embroidery can take years to complete and are often worked on by more than one person. Suzhou, Hunan, Sichuan, and Guangdong are the embroidery centers of China. These regions have their own designs and styles. One of the most famous is the double-sided embroidery where the same image, or more unusually a different one, appears on the reverse side. The stitches of some pieces of embroidery are so fine that it is hard to tell one stitch from the next, and they look like paintings.

INTERNET LINKS

www.china-on-site.com/pages/comic/1.php
An illustrated story of the Monkey King is presented on this website.

www.firstpalette.com/Craft_themes/World/Chinese_Opera_Mask/Chinese_Opera_Mask.html
This website provides downloadable templates of Chinese opera masks that you can color and complete.

LEISURE

A group of elderly Chinese practicing tai chi on the Bund Promenade in Shanghai.

11

MANY RECREATIONAL ACTIVITIES in China are concentrated around relaxing in the park, taking part in martial arts and sports, or playing games.

FUN IN THE PARK

Parks in urban China are seldom empty. As early as 5 A.M., the parks fill up with people. Most are the elderly who start their day with a session of *taijiquan* (tie-chi-chuan) or qigong, both martial-art forms, usually done in a group. Under the current labor law, men retire at 60 and women at 55. That leaves them a lot of time to enjoy board games and exercise in the park with fellow retirees.

Chinese people dancing in the Temple of Heaven Park in Beijing.

A Chinese girl playing jump rope.

People will join whoever is in motion; sometimes half of the park is filled with strangers united in exercise. In the summer months some people may switch to aerobics.

Parks are also filled with birdsong. The most popular bird is the Chinese thrush. Birds are kept in round, beautifully carved cages. Their cages are hung from the branches of trees, and the birds sing in competition with one another. Many Chinese keep birds as pets, although in the cities there are more pet cats and dogs. Dogs need a government license.

On Sundays groups of opera lovers and musicians gather in the parks to give impromptu performances. A person could start playing a fiddle while a passerby bursts into song, followed by another. When everything is over, they go their separate ways and may never perform together again.

Families also go to the park on Sundays for a walk. The Chinese love posing for and taking photographs. They often pose with flowers, plants, statues, or anything else that might make a good picture, sometimes waiting in line for a photograph of a commemorative statue or display.

CHILDREN'S GAMES

Children in China play most of the same games as children elsewhere in the world. Hopscotch, jump rope, marbles, and cat's cradle are all popular schoolyard games, while computer games are also catching on.

Boys also play a game with a heavy-base shuttlecock. They stand in a circle kicking the shuttlecock around trying to keep it up. In another game, a boy stands in the middle of a circle, tosses a ball high into the air, and shouts the name of a friend. The named person must catch the ball, go into the circle, and repeat the process. The person who fails to catch the ball or come to the center when his name is called is hit with the ball. This can be a painful game, but it is lots of fun.

THE STORYTELLER

Chinese storytellers perform to audiences of all ages. They entertain with epics, classics, martial-arts stories, and contemporary stories. The props, if any, are simple—a fan, a table, a chair. The storyteller makes a wide sweep with the fan and tells of soldiers thundering across the desert. The fan may also be a coy lady's accessory, or it could be slapped against the body to show the tyranny of an emperor. The table, likewise, could become the front of a bus, a magistrate's table, a counter in a department store, or a hospital bed.

The magic lies in the storytellers' skill. They change not only the tone of their voice to assume a different character but their expressions and behavior as well. The beauty of it all is the audience never mixes up the characters or train of events.

This profession started out with itinerant storytellers who moved from village to village providing entertainment. Some would light a joss stick and time the story so that the most exciting part ended when the joss stick finished. A hat was passed around and the story would continue. Audiences laughed, cried, and trembled in fear with the storyteller.

Many variety shows onstage and on television now include a storyteller. Another form of entertainment has evolved from this. Called crosstalk, it involves two or more performers playing out a comic script like standup comics of the West.

Girls play with a thick rope made of rubber bands. It is stretched between two girls, while the rest take turns jumping in and out, twisting and turning, making patterns with the rope. The rope starts at the ankles of the two girls at either end and is raised higher and higher with each turn, making jumping over it more and more difficult.

Children in the countryside play simple games with whatever they can find. There is a game they play with pieces of paper the size of playing cards. If paper is not available, they use leaves. Each person has his or her share with one piece put in the center. The children then take turns trying to flip over the paper or leaf by slapping their own paper or leaf down near it. If the air current they produce succeeds in doing that, they get to keep the paper or leaf in the center.

MARTIAL ARTS

Taijiquan and qigong are usually performed in the early morning. It is believed that practicing these exercises at this time will reap the most benefits to one's body.

A group of Chinese women practicing *taijiquan* with swords in Victoria Park in Hong Kong.

TAIJIQUAN Practiced by the Chinese since the 17th century, *taijiquan* is made up of hundreds of positions originally used in self-defense. It is also known as shadowboxing, for smooth, graceful, circular movements are combined with deep breathing and performed with concentration. Perhaps the most beneficial feeling is the calmness that comes after the exercises.

Taijiquan has its origins in the preparation for combat. Controlled breathing and slow, circular body movements ensure that all the limbs and internal organs are exercised.

Taijiquan had only eight primary hand gestures and five body movements when it was invented. More movements were added through the years, and now there are five major styles of *taijiquan*. More recently developed styles include quick movements with lively footwork and movements borrowed from fencing.

QIGONG This is a deep-breathing exercise that regulates the mind and the body. The aim of qigong is to achieve longevity. With breath control and concentration, chi can be directed to various parts of the body to increase strength and decrease pain. Some people use this skill to perform feats like lying under the wheels of a moving car or bending iron bars.

Qigong is used more as a therapeutic form of physical exercise than for amazing acts. It has been proven useful in controlling high blood pressure, heart disease, aches and pains, and breathing disorders. Therapeutic qigong can be done lying down, sitting, standing, or walking. It emphasizes calming the mind, concentration, and regulating breathing. A combination of these stimulates the nervous system, increases blood circulation and metabolism, and puts the body on the road to self-renewal.

WUSHU This art of fighting is thousands of years old. The four main categories are Chinese boxing with bare hands, duet boxing, swordplay, and group exercise.

The most popular form of wushu is Chinese boxing, seen in kung fu movies, where hands and legs move lightning fast, with long, high jumps. Of the many forms of Chinese boxing, one is based on strength, while another requires cunning. The latter imitates the movements of 12 animals such as the dragon, the tiger, the monkey, the horse, the snake, the eagle, the sparrow, the turtle, and even the praying mantis. Yet another form of Chinese boxing imitates drunkenness with such variations as the Eight Drunken Immortals or the Drunken Monkey.

Weapons used in wushu include the saber, the spear, the sword, clubs, and the nine-link chain. Students of wushu perform it for the beauty and exercise of the art rather than for fighting.

People playing ping-pong at tables set up in the park for public use.

SPORTS

All forms of sports are popular in China. Schools, factories, and large organizations often have sporting facilities such as basketball and badminton courts and ping-pong tables. Some organizations reserve 10 or 20 minutes a day for mass exercises. As part of an emphasis on sports, which was especially strong in the mid-20th century, the government funds and trains young talented players in the hopes that they will become professional players.

Because of its relative simplicity, inexpensive equipment, and accessibility, badminton is a very established and popular sport in China. Amateur leagues exist across the country. Ping-pong, basketball, and volleyball are other favorites. China has produced some of the best international players in these sports.

Dragon-boat racing dates back about 2,000 years and remains a traditional event held throughout China every year.

BOARD GAMES

In a city park or a quiet village square in the evening, men seated on low stools concentrate over a chessboard. They are playing elephant chess or weiqi *(way-chee), both strategy board games.*

Elephant chess, or xiangqi *(shiang-chee), has been around since* A.D. *700. Chess pieces include cannons, elephants, cavalry, infantry, and chariots, with a fortress in which the king and his counselors are entrenched. The two halves of the chessboard are separated by the Yellow River. The objective is to storm the enemy's fortress and capture the king, who never leaves the fortress. Chessmen travel along lines, like in* weiqi.

Weiqi, or Go, is the oldest board game in China, having been around for thousands of years. Wei means "to surround," and qi means "board game." It is played on a grid board marked with 19 vertical and 19 horizontal lines using 181 black and 180 white flat, round counters. Players mark out their own territories and then try to capture each other's men and territory. Single or whole groups of men can be captured and removed from the board. The winner is the one who has gained the most territory and men. Weiqi is considered the most complicated board game in the world because of the high number of possible moves.

Thanks in large part to substantial government support, China is a major chess power, with 30 Grandmasters and 21 Woman Grandmasters in total. Grandmaster is the highest title a chess player can attain, and it is awarded by the World Chess Federation. Currently five of the world's top 100 players, including the reigning Women's World Chess Champion, Hou Yifan, are from China.

Mah-jongg is a game that originated in China, commonly played by four players (with some three-player variations found in Korea and Japan). Similar to the Western card game rummy, mah-jongg is a game of skill, strategy, and calculation and involves a certain degree of chance. In Asia mah-jongg is also popularly played as a gambling game. The game is played with a set of 136 tiles based on Chinese characters and symbols, although some regional variations use a different number of tiles. It remains far more popular in Asia than in the West.

Ping-pong played an important part in restoring diplomatic relations between China and the United States. In a move known later as "ping-pong diplomacy," China invited a United States team to China in 1971, helping to mend a 20-year rift. The Chinese play ping-pong anywhere, both indoors and outdoors, on any surface on which a ping-pong ball can bounce.

Yao Ming is a former professional basketball player from China who last played for the Houston Rockets of the National Basketball Association (NBA). When he retired in 2011 he was, at 7 feet 6 inches (2.29 m), the tallest player in the NBA. Yao Ming's success contributed to the growing popularity of basketball in the world's most populated country. Some experts estimate as many as 300 million of China's 1.3 billion population now play basketball.

In warmer weather, many Chinese swim in rivers and canals, disregarding "no swimming" signs. In winter, northerners use the same rivers and canals for ice-skating.

Among China's minorities, sporting activities include Mongolian-style wrestling and horsemanship, Tibetan yak races, Korean springboarding, and the Miaos' crossbow events.

Relatively obscure winter sports such as bandy (Russian hockey) and curling are also popular in the northern regions.

Ping-pong is one of the most popular amateur sports in China today, with an estimated 200 million players.

INTERNET LINKS

www.childbook.com/Chinese-Children-Game-Instructions-s/79.htm

This website offers myriad traditional Chinese games for kids with free and printable instructions.

www.shaolins.com/encyclopedia/

This website provides many interesting pictures of Shaolin kung fu.

www.yaoming.net/

Everything you could possibly want to know about China's basketball superstar Yao Ming is provided in this website.

FESTIVALS

Red lanterns hanging over a street, lending the atmosphere a more festive feel during Chinese New Year.

12

THE CHINESE CALENDAR is basically an agricultural one that charts changes in season, temperature, rainfall, and growing cycle. It follows the passage of the moon and divides the year into 12 lunar months.

This does not coincide with the Gregorian calendar followed by Western countries. Although the Western calendar has been adopted for daily use, some of the older generation use the Chinese calendar more than the Western one because it marks the seasons more accurately.

MAJOR FESTIVALS

LUNAR NEW YEAR   Falling on the first day of the first lunar month, this is the most important festival for the Chinese in China and all around the world. It usually takes place between late January and late February and marks the beginning of spring, so it is also known as the Spring Festival.

Preparations start with spring cleaning and decorating the home with symbols of good luck. New clothes are bought, rice bins are filled to the brim, larders are stocked, quarrels are mended, and debts are paid.

The most important event of the New Year preparations is the reunion dinner. Children, no matter how far from home, make special efforts to be home with their parents on New Year's Eve. Certain foods are a must on the table. For example, in the north, *jiao zi* (chi-ao zher), or dumplings, are shaped like gold ingots to represent wealth.

At midnight on New Year's Eve, firecrackers are set off to scare away any evil spirits. All lights in the house are turned on to chase away bad

The traditional Chinese holidays are an essential part of Chinese culture. Many holidays are associated with Chinese mythology and folklore, but they probably originated from ancient farmer rituals for celebrating harvests or prayer offerings.

A dance troupe performs during Chinese New Year celebrations in Beijing.

luck. On the first day of the new year, people dress in new clothes to visit relatives. Children kneel and pay their respects to their elders. In return, they receive little red packets with money inside. Nothing unpleasant is allowed to happen on this day, to ensure good fortune for the rest of the year.

Chunyun is a period of travel in China around the time of the Chinese New Year with extremely high traffic. The period usually begins 15 days before Lunar New Year's Day and lasts for around 40 days. The number of passenger journeys during Chunyun has exceeded the population of China, hitting more than 2 billion in 2008. It is the largest annual human migration in the world. Some trains are so crowded that using the lavatory is impossible, and there are reports of migrant workers traveling home wearing adult diapers because there is no toilet access. In fact, supermarkets have reported a 50 percent increase in sales of adult diapers during that time.

QINGMING JIE The Clear and Bright Festival comes around in early spring. On this day the Chinese remember their dead ancestors, visiting cemeteries to sweep the ancestors' tombs clean and pay respects to them. This is not a solemn day as one would imagine. Burial grounds are usually in the countryside, so visits to the cemetery are turned into family outings. Picnics and activities such as kite flying make these visits a festive affair.

ZHONGQIU JIE The 15th day of the eighth lunar month marks the time when the moon is at its fullest and brightest. This is when the Chinese celebrate the Mid-Autumn Festival. The fall weather is at its best, and people come out at night to admire the moon and enjoy the weather.

Mooncakes made of a thin pastry filled with sweet mashed lotus seeds are eaten and given as gifts. The night is also filled with lights from paper lanterns. Children are busy looking for the lady in the moon, having often heard the legend about how she got there. The legend says that a lady named Chang'e was married to a tyrannical king. He had a potion that could make him immortal. Fearing for her people, Chang'e stole the potion and drank it. She became immortal and immediately flew to the moon, where she has been ever since.

Dragon-boat racing is a noisy and exciting affair.

DUANWU JIE This festival is held on the fifth day of the fifth lunar month and is known as the Dragon Boat Festival. It is held to remember a patriotic poet who drowned himself because his state was taken over by a neighboring state. Villagers rushed to the river and threw in rice dumplings to prevent the fish from eating his body. They spent days in a boat trying to recover his body; all they had to eat were rice dumplings filled with meat and wrapped in bamboo leaves. To remember this day, dragon-boat races are held and rice dumplings are eaten.

MINORITY FESTIVALS

TIBETAN BATHING FESTIVAL Between late summer and early fall, Tibetans celebrate the Bathing Festival, or Gamariji, which refers to the planet Venus. As Venus rises in the sky, the mass bathing begins. The festival lasts for seven days until the star is out of sight.

Legend has it that during an epidemic, the goddess of mercy, Guanyin, sent down seven fairies with seven bottles of holy water to be put into the rivers, lakes, and ponds of Tibet. That night, everyone in Tibet dreamed that a girl covered in sores bathed in a river and was immediately cured. The next morning, all the sick people rushed to bathe in the rivers and were cured. Tibetans now celebrate the festival by bathing and washing their clothes in rivers. While the clothes line the banks of rivers to dry, their owners indulge their festive mood by drinking copious amounts of barley wine and buttered tea.

DAI WATER SPLASHING FESTIVAL The Dai minority of Yunnan celebrate the second day of their New Year by splashing water on each other. This is done to shower blessings and to wish for happiness: the more water, the more wishes. This means buckets of fun. The elderly are the only ones spared. Ladles of water are poured down people's backs, or drops of water from wet olive branches are sprinkled on their heads while good wishes are uttered. It is the most important festival observed by the Dai ethnic people of Xishuangbanna Prefecture and is similar to neighboring Thailand's Songkran Festival.

The Dai people of Yunnan usher in the new year by splashing water on one another.

PUBLIC HOLIDAYS

China has fewer public holidays than most other countries in the world. But these include three one-week holiday periods for the Spring Festival and National Day (October 1). The Chinese New Year is three days long. The weeklong holidays began in 2000 as a means of increasing and encouraging holiday spending. They are called "golden weeks" and have become peak seasons for travel and tourism. In 2008 the Labor Day holiday was shortened to one day, and three traditional Chinese holidays were added.

National Day is one of the grandest public celebrations in China. Beijing celebrates with elaborate fireworks and mass-formation dances at Tiananmen Square.

If a public holiday falls early in the week, the Chinese prefer to work on Sunday and take Monday and Tuesday off.

Some holidays are for only certain groups of people. On March 8, International Working Women's Day, Chinese women get a half-day off from work. International Children's Day on June 1 means no school. May 4 is Chinese Youth Day, when older children get a half-day off from school.

INTERNET LINKS

http://traditions.cultural-china.com/en/14Traditions68.html
This website provides a description of the Dragon Boat Festival, complete with pictures.

www.china.org.cn/english/features/Festivals/78311.htm
This website explains the Mid-Autumn Festival in words and pictures.

www.travelchinaguide.com/intro/social_customs/zodiac/
On this website you can read about the Chinese zodiac as well as find out about your own Chinese zodiac sign and horoscope.

FOOD

Fresh produce for sale at a market in Hong Kong.

13

A DAILY ACTIVITY THAT THE CHINESE most enjoy is eating. *"Chi le ma?"* (cheh leh mah), meaning "Have you eaten yet?" often follows *"Ni hao"* (ni how), meaning "Hello" or "How are you?" Sometimes people do not even say hello but just ask whether you have had a meal.

Poverty led the Chinese to develop unique styles of cooking. Stir-frying food cut up into small, even pieces that cook quickly saved precious firewood, as did braising and simmering soups on the same fire used to warm the house. To make full use of an animal that was killed for food, the Chinese invented a recipe for every part of the animal except the fur or the feathers.

KITCHEN ESSENTIALS

The Chinese cook their food on burners fueled by firewood in the country and gas in the city. The kitchen may have a few fancy appliances, the most popular being the electric rice cooker. The most important kitchen tools are a cleaver, a wok, a soup ladle, and a pair of chopsticks.

The Chinese cleaver is a heavy knife with a broad, rectangular blade. Kept razor-sharp, it can hack hard bones and slice and shred meat and vegetables very finely. The flat side of the cleaver is used to bruise ginger and garlic, whereas the blunt edge tenderizes meat and knocks out live fish. The end of the handle is used to crush garlic and mash black beans.

The Chinese feel that chopsticks reflect gentleness and benevolence, the main moral teaching of Confucianism. Another reason they use chopsticks is that most Chinese food is stir-fried and cut into small pieces.

Rice is so important to the Chinese that fan *(fun), meaning "rice," refers to a whole meal. Many Chinese sayings revolve around rice. The breadwinner is one who "puts rice on the table," whereas to "break someone's rice bowl" means to make another lose his or her job. If a Chinese asks you to come and eat rice, he or she is inviting you to a meal.*

Rice is treated with utmost respect. Every spilled grain is picked up, washed, and cooked. Parents persuade their children to eat up every grain of rice in their bowl by telling them that a bowl dotted with rice grains means they will marry someone with pockmarked skin. Fan *is eaten with* cai *(chai), a general term for dishes that accompany rice.*

An unusual rice recipe is exploded rice. Uncooked rice is put into a drum that is heated over charcoal to a high temperature. It is rotated, and when a certain amount of pressure is reached, a valve is released, and with a bang, the rice grains spill out into a waiting bag. The grains look and taste like Rice Krispies and are eaten as a snack or pressed together with sweet syrup to make a cookie.

The wok is an all-purpose cooking utensil. The best woks are made of cast iron, but it is common to find woks in stainless steel, aluminum, or a nonstick material. The wok is a half-sphere with a handle on either side. It is used for deep-frying, shallow frying, stir-frying, boiling, and simmering. Sometimes a pair of chopsticks are placed across the bottom over water, and a bowl is balanced on them to steam food inside the bowl.

REGIONAL CUISINE

BEIJING CUISINE   This northern cuisine is characterized by the liberal use of garlic and chilies. Food is often drenched in oil and seasoned with vinegar, salt, and sugar. Less rice is eaten in the north, as wheat grows better in the drier weather. Plain steamed buns or wheat pancakes are eaten as a staple, with stir-fried dishes of diced meat and vegetables or stewed meats. Wheat

CHOPSTICKS

Chinese started eating with chopsticks 3,000 years ago. They were probably invented to pick up bite-size pieces of food. Soldiers going to war had a special kit consisting of a cutting knife and a pair of chopsticks. Regular chopsticks are tapered, slim objects with a blunt end. They are about 8 inches (20.3 cm) long, though those used for cooking may be 2 feet (0.6 m) long.

Chopsticks are usually made of wood, bamboo, or plastic. The more elaborate ones have cloisonné designs or are made of ivory or jade. Emperors ate with silver chopsticks that they believed would turn black if the food were poisoned.

Chinese use chopsticks to eat everything except soup. They use chopsticks to push rice from the bowl into the mouth, to pick up portions of food, and even to eat cake! Children start using chopsticks as soon as they can hold a pair and coordinate their movements. There is no rule as to how they should be used, except that they should never cross.

dumplings stuffed with minced meat and vegetables are eaten as a main meal, especially in winter.

Beijing food also includes dishes from neighboring Mongolia. One of the most popular is skewered mutton. Sold along the streets, skewered mutton is fried in oil and rolled in powdered chili and cumin. Mongolian rinsed mutton is also popular. Diners sit around a charcoal-heated funneled pot, dipping thin slices of mutton into the hot water. The barely cooked meat is then dipped into a fermented bean-curd sauce and eaten with Chinese cabbage and thin noodles.

SHANGHAI CUISINE This cuisine is eaten throughout the lower Yangtze River Delta. This region is known as the Land of Rice and Fish, and its cuisine revolves around whatever can be caught in the rivers. Fish, eels, and shrimp are steamed or cooked in tasty soy- and sugar-based sauces. Another favorite condiment is black vinegar, which is used as a dip or in a sauce. As in northern

cuisine, a lot of oil and chilies are used, and the simple cooking methods bring out the best flavor of the food.

SICHUAN CUISINE Sichuan has the spiciest food in China. Most dishes are covered in a red chili oil and sprinkled with a potent, fragrant pepper. This pepper has a delayed numbing effect on the tongue that can deaden all sense of taste for several seconds.

As fish is hard to come by in Sichuan, pork, beef, and eggplant are more usually cooked in a fish-flavored

Chinese having a meal at a traditional teahouse in Sichuan, which is known for its spicy cuisine.

sauce that is actually a mixture of vinegar, hot bean paste, ginger, garlic, and scallions.

Other Sichuan specialties include camphor-and-tea-smoked duck, where the bird is slowly smoked over a fire of camphor chips and tea leaves. The fragrant duck is then deep-fried and eaten with a thick, sweet soy sauce. *Dan dan* (dahn dahn) noodles are also a favorite. Cold boiled noodles are tossed into a bowl and seasoned with chili oil, ginger juice, garlic paste, soy sauce, vinegar, and sugar. Sometimes this is topped with shreds of cucumber and sesame-seed paste.

CANTONESE CUISINE This is the best-known form of Chinese cuisine outside China. The Cantonese are known to be very fussy about the freshness of the ingredients in their dishes. Dishes are never overcooked, and flavors are seldom masked with heavy, spicy, or pungent sauces. Vegetables are lightly stir-fried or blanched in hot water and dressed with oyster sauce.

The Cantonese are also famous for their thin egg noodles, which are eaten with a dumpling soup or topped with roasted meats. Soups are an integral part of Cantonese cuisine. Sometimes boiled with traditional Chinese herbs, these soups are simmered for hours over a charcoal fire.

CHINESE EXOTICA

"If it moves and its back faces the sun, the Chinese will eat it." The Cantonese are especially famous for their exotic taste in meat. Snake is made into a thick soup, while dog is roasted or stewed. Hard-to-find iguanas are suspended in wine and eaten in small amounts for their tonic effect. Chinese believe that the more exotic the meat, the better it is for one's health. For example, dried pieces of crocodile meat made into a soup are said to do wonders for a child's cough.

Bear paws are now hard to find, but when they are available, they are braised and served to very important guests. Braised camel hooves, another delicacy, have a gelatinous texture and no particular taste. Fortunately or unfortunately, the Chinese camel has two humps. Braised in stock, these humps look and taste like lumps of fat. Camels' noses are not spared either. Since each camel has only one nose, they are a much rarer delicacy.

Other delicacies include bird's nests—that is, the dried mucus from a swallow's salivary glands that the bird uses to line its home. Served in sweet or savory soups, bird's nests are regarded as a tonic. Shark fins are made into a rich, thick soup, whereas sea slugs and jellyfish are prepared in a variety of ways.

Century eggs start as fresh eggs covered in an alkaline ash and kept for a month or longer in a cool dark place. By that time, the egg white has turned into a black jelly, and the yellow yolk is ringed with gray. They are often eaten as an appetizer with vinegar or pickled ginger.

OODLES OF NOODLES

Noodles, or *mien* (mi-an) in Chinese, come in all shapes, sizes, and lengths. In the north, they are made of plain wheat and water and look like flat spaghetti. They can be eaten plain, dressed in garlic, chilies, and vinegar, boiled in a plain soup, or fried with chives and soy sauce.

In western China, *shou mien* (show mi-an), or hand noodles, and *la mien* (lah mi-an), or pulled noodles, are more popular. Hand noodles are made

with the same wheat-and-water dough, but the noodles are formed by plucking bits of dough and throwing them into boiling water. With pulled noodles, bits of dough are pulled into thick lengths before being boiled. Both types of noodles are fried in a tomato-based sauce with onions, bell peppers, and bits of mutton.

In Shanxi Province, cut noodles are a specialty. Lumps of dough are held in the hand, and slices are cut off into a boiling pot of water. Master noodle makers are so skilled that they balance lumps of dough on their hats while they slice off pieces with knives held in each hand.

A chef makes la mien *by literally pulling it.*

In the south, eggs are added to the wheat dough. Sometimes a few drops of alkaline water are added to give the noodles a slightly bitter but pleasant taste. Rice flour is also used to make noodles in the south. Noodles there are round or flat and can be as thick as spaghetti or as fine as hair. They are fried soft or crispy, topped with a hearty sauce of shrimp and pork, or added to a rich soup.

Long noodles symbolize a long life and are served at birthday celebrations.

BANQUETS

Chinese banquets are lengthy, noisy meals that leave one absolutely stuffed with food. Snacks such as peanuts, candied walnuts, or pickled cabbage are served before the meal starts. Sometimes cold cuts will be laid on the table before the guests arrive.

There are usually 10 guests at each round table. At each setting is a small saucer for soy sauce, a plate, a small bowl, a pair of chopsticks, a spoon, and some glasses for soft drinks and alcoholic beverages.

Dinner starts with hors d'oeuvres, a mixture of hot and cold dishes such as seasoned jellyfish and century eggs. The platter is often elaborately decorated with the food making geometric designs or forming part of a peacock's tail. Guests usually help themselves, and the host will always make sure that their plates are constantly full.

Dishes are served one at a time, to be admired before being consumed. There are usually 10 dishes at a banquet. The next-to-last dish is usually a soup to wash everything down, followed by fried rice or noodles to "fill the stomach" just in case one did not have enough. Dessert at the end may be a flaky pastry filled with mashed beans or nuts, a sweet soup of whole beans, or nuts and a fruit platter.

The most elaborate of Chinese banquets is the emperor's banquet, which consists of 132 courses, all at one sitting. No wonder the Chinese equivalent for "bon appétit" is *man man chi* (mun-mun-cheh), meaning "please eat slowly" and savor your food.

When Chinese eat out, the decor of the restaurant is often the least important factor. Most Chinese restaurants are simply furnished with bare essentials.

HOME-COOKED MEALS

Chinese are particular about the freshness of their food, so shopping for fresh ingredients, especially vegetables, is a daily affair. They buy whatever foods are in season. In the north, for example, meals in winter use Chinese cabbage. This hardy vegetable is grown in the fall and survives the bitterly cold winter. Outer leaves are removed to reveal fresh, crispy leaves within.

Breakfast is usually a thin porridge made from leftover rice or broken rice grains too small to make a good pot of rice. It is eaten with a wide variety of pickled vegetables or pieces of salty fermented bean curd. In the south, meat and eggs are added to the porridge to make a tasty dish called congee. Fried dough sticks, unleavened bread sprinkled with sesame seeds, or noodles are sometimes eaten.

Dinner is the main meal of the day and is eaten early, between 5 and 6 P.M. Family members sit around a table filled with dishes. The soup is usually placed in the middle, surrounded by two or three dishes of vegetables and a main dish of fish, poultry, or pork. Family members have a bowl of rice each and help themselves from the common dishes.

A Chinese woman cooking a meal in her kitchen.

Chinese cooking is a balance of contrasting tastes and textures. There will never be two sweet-sour dishes or two deep-fried dishes on the same table. Soups are served as part of a meal and are used to cleanse and refresh the palate during the meal.

TABLE MANNERS

Do not be surprised if a Chinese eats noisily at the table. It is not considered bad manners to slurp soup, although it is poor upbringing if one chews noisily. Using chopsticks as drumsticks on the table is disrespectful. Chopsticks are also never used to point at a person or gesticulate with during a conversation.

A meal starts only when everyone is seated. Children invite their elders to eat before starting their own meals. Usually a mouthful of plain rice is eaten first before any of the other dishes are touched. A person helps himself or herself to the nearest dish first. Food taken from any dish must be from the part of the plate nearest the person. Morsels of food must be taken from the top. It is rude to flip over pieces of food or take pieces from the bottom of the plate. A person also never chooses the best pieces, which are offered to the oldest person at the table or to a guest.

Chinese think it is perfectly all right to put the bones on the table. In some restaurants, bones are even deposited on the floor.

WHAT'S IN A NAME?

Chinese get very poetic about the names of their dishes. Reading a menu is sometimes like reading a fairy tale; no food is mentioned, only phoenixes, jade stalks, and lion's heads. Spinach served with boiled bean curd is known as Red-Beaked Green Parrots on White Marble, whereas a Lion's Head is a meatball the size of a baseball.

Ants Crawling Up a Tree Trunk is less dangerous than one may think. It is only ground meat cooked with transparent bean noodles. Pockmarked Bean Curd sounds unappetizing but is named after a woman with unfortunate skin who invented the dish of bean curd cooked with minced meat and hot broad-bean paste. This dish, with white pieces of bean curd swimming in a sauce red with chili oil and bits of minced pork, does look like a skin problem.

Red-Cooked Water Paddles are quite tasty, consisting of fish fins cooked in a soybean sauce. Drunken Chicken is cold chicken marinated in wine. Beggar's Chicken has a more colorful background. A beggar once stole a chicken and, afraid of being discovered, coated it with mud, feathers and all, and threw it into a fire. When the coast was clear, he cracked open the hardened mud and found that the chicken was fragrant and delicious.

Monk Jumps Over the Wall is one of the most expensive dishes one can order. It consists of all sorts of dried seafood stewed slowly in a clay pot. The story goes that a meditating monk was distracted by a wonderful aroma wafting over a wall. After a while, he could not stand it any longer and jumped over the wall to ask for a taste.

WINE

Chinese wines are made from rice, sorghum, millet, or grapes that are naturally fermented. The most popular wines are made from rice. The three main types of wine are white wine, yellow wine, and burning wine, which is high in alcohol.

White wine is made from glutinous rice and is light and sweet. Yellow wine is also made from rice and has a stronger flavor, turning darker with age. Chinese spirits are potent, often colorless liquids that can make one's mouth and stomach seem on fire. The Chinese like to drink their wine warm and in small cups, which they empty in one gulp.

There are many stories about Chinese wine. One of the most famous Chinese poets, Li Bai, is said to have written his best pieces while intoxicated. Many of his poems speak of the joys of wine and the wonderful companion it makes. He is believed to have drowned while trying to rescue the moon. In his drunken state, he thought it had fallen in the lake.

Another tale tells of an emperor's forgotten pot of rice that fermented into wine. It tasted so good that there was a tasting party that left everyone with a hangover. The emperor then decreed that wine should always be drunk from tiny cups, that it must always be taken with food, and that mild mental or physical exercise should be performed when drinking wine.

In Shaoxing, famous for its yellow wine, a father seals and buries an earthen jar of good wine the day his daughter is born. This wine is unearthed when the girl marries and is used as part of her wedding celebrations. Chinese "yellow liquor" is sometimes distilled for a more potent alcoholic drink called *baijiu* (buy-jew), or "white liquor," which can have an alcohol content as high as 80 percent.

TEA

Tea is the most important beverage in China. It is drunk at all times of the day instead of water. In ancient China it was used for medicinal purposes, and

Tea is an integral part of any Chinese meal.

modern Chinese still swear by it. They believe it stimulates the digestive and nervous systems and the heart, reduces the harmful effects of smoking and alcohol, and reduces fat.

Most of China's tea grows in the south. The finest teas are found growing on mist-covered cliffs so high up that trained monkeys are used to pluck them.

There are three types of tea: green, red, and oolong, or black dragon. Green tea is a light refreshing drink made from dried young tea leaves. Red tea is made from leaves that have been fermented and toasted, making a stronger, more flavorful tea. Oolong tea is made from partially fermented leaves and is the most widely drunk tea in China and abroad. Sometimes jasmine flowers are added in the fermentation process of green or oolong tea to perfume it.

Everyday tea is made by adding hot water to a spoonful of leaves; with additions of water the leaves last the whole day. The water should just come to a boil before it is poured into a warmed teapot holding the tea leaves. The tea is allowed to stand for three to five minutes and is drunk from porcelain cups. Tea connoisseurs make their tea in tiny brown clay teapots that hold about a tablespoon of leaves. Hot water is added to the leaves and then thrown away. The second addition of hot water brings out the flavor of the tea.

In Chinese society the younger generation always shows its respect to the older generation by offering a cup of tea. Inviting and paying for their elders to go to restaurants for tea is a traditional activity on holidays.

INTERNET LINKS

http://eatingchina.com/index.htm
This website features cooking tips, recipes, and history about certain Chinese foods.

www.foreigners-in-china.com/chinese-wok.html
This website provides an elaborate account of how to use the wok, complete with videos showing how to fry rice.

PEKING DUCK

Peking Duck, also known as Peking Roast Duck, is a famous dish from Beijing.

Large pot of water

1 whole duck, giblets removed

1 teaspoon (5 ml) freshly ground white pepper

1 teaspoon (5 ml) sesame oil

2 teaspoons (10 ml) peanut oil

½ teaspoon (2.5 ml) ground star anise

¾ cup (180 ml) red-wine vinegar

1½ tablespoons (22.5 ml) ground cinnamon

1½ tablespoons (22.5 ml) ground ginger

¾ cup (180 ml) brown sugar

Bring water to the boil. Remove it from the stove, and lower the duck into the water. Leave for five minutes. Remove duck and pat dry. Combine the other ingredients in a small saucepan and bring to a boil. Turn off the heat, and leave the mixture to cool to room temperature. Liberally coat the duck with the mixture, and leave it to sit at room temperature for three hours so that the coating dries out. Place duck on a rack, breast side up, in a preheated 350°F (177°C) oven for 2–2½ hours. Roast until skin is crisp and brown. Check occasionally and regulate the temperature so that the coating does not burn. Leave duck to cool to room temperature. Carefully carve pieces from the bone, being sure to include some of the crisp skin with each piece.

BRAISED CHICKEN

Braised chicken is a traditional dish from Dezhou.

1 whole chicken
2 scallion stalks
2 or 3 slices of fresh gingerroot
4 tablespoons (60 ml) oil
3 tablespoons (45 ml) sherry
½ cup (125 ml) oyster sauce*
2 cups (500 ml) water
½ teaspoon (2.5 ml) salt
6 dried black mushrooms, soaked in water
6 Chinese red dates*
1 tablespoon (15 ml) sugar
1 Chinese parsley

With a cleaver, chop chicken into 1½- to 2-inch (3.8- to 5.1-cm) pieces. Trim scallion stalks and slice gingerroot. Heat oil in a large heavy pan, and brown chicken pieces quickly. Add scallion stalks, gingerroot, sherry, oyster sauce, water, and salt. Bring to a boil, then cover and simmer for 20–30 minutes. Add black mushrooms, red dates, and sugar. Simmer for another 10–15 minutes. Transfer chicken pieces to a serving bowl. Strain sauce and pour over chicken. Garnish with Chinese parsley and serve.

*Oyster sauce and Chinese red dates can be purchased in a grocery store specializing in Chinese foods.

MAP OF CHINA

E

Anhui, D3

Beijing, D2
Bangladesh, B4
Bay of Bengal, A4—C4
Bhutan, B3
Bohai Sea, D2

Changchun, E2
Changde, D3
Chengdu, C3

East China Sea, E3

Fujian, D3—D4
Fuzhou, D4

Gansu, B2, C2—C3
Gobi Desert, C2—D2
Guangdong, D4
Guangxi, C4
Guangzhou, D4
Guilin, C4
Guiyang, C3
Guizhou, C3—C4

Haikou, D4
Hainan, C4—D4
Hangzhou, D3
Harbin, E2
Hebei, D2—D3
Hefei, D3
Heilongjiang, D1, E1—E2
Henan, D3
Hohhot, D2
Hong Kong SAR, D4
Huang He, C2—C3, D2
Hubei, C3—D3
Hunan, C3, D3—D4

India, A3—A4, B4
Inner, Mongolia D2

Ji'an, D3
Jiangsu, D3
Jiangxi, D3—D4

Jilin, D2—E2
Jinan, D3

Kazakhstan, A1—A2, B1
Kunming, C4
Kyrgystan, A2

Lanzhou, C3
Laos, C4
Lhasa, B3
Liaoning, D2—E2

Mongolia, B1—B2, C1—C2, D1, D2
Mt. Everest, B3
Myanmar (Burma), B3—B4, C3—C4

Nanjing, D3
Nanning, C4
Nepal, A3—B3
Ningde, D3
Ningxia, C2—C3
North Korea, E2

Qinghai, B2—B3, C2—C3

Russia, A1—D1

Shaanxi, C3, D2—D3
Shandong, D2—D3
Shanghai, D3
Shanxi, D2—D3

Shenyang, E2
Sichuan, C3
South China Sea, C4—D4
South Korea, E2—E3

Taipei, D4
Taiwan, D4
Taiyuan, D2
Taklimakan Desert, A2
Thailand, C4
Tianjin, D2
Turpan Depression, B2

Urumqi, B2

Vietnam, C4

Wuhan, D3

Xi River, C4—D4
Xi'an, C3
Xining, C3
Xinjiang, A2—A3, B1—B3
Xizang (Tibet), A3—C3

Yangquan, D2
Yangtze River, C3
Yellow Sea, D3—E3
Yinchuan, C2

Zhejiang, D3
Zhengzhou, D3

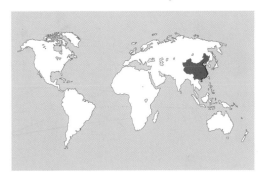

ECONOMIC CHINA

Agriculture

 Cotton

 Rice

 Tea

 Wheat

Manufacturing

 Aircraft

 Silk

 Steel

 Textiles

 Vehicles

Natural Resources

CP Copper

 Coal

 Gold

 Hydroelectricity

 Oil and natural gas

ABOUT THE ECONOMY

OVERVIEW

The People's Republic of China is the world's second-largest economy, after the United States. It is the world's fastest-growing major economy, with average annual growth rates of about 10 percent for the past 30 years. China is also the largest exporter and second-largest importer of goods in the world. China became the world's top manufacturer in 2011, surpassing the United States.

GROSS DOMESTIC PRODUCT (GDP)

$5.88 trillion (2010)

GDP SECTORS

Agriculture: 9.6 percent; industry: 46.8 percent; service: 43.6 percent (2010)

WORKFORCE

780 million (2010 estimate)

INFLATION RATE

5 percent (2010 estimate)

CURRENCY

US$1 = ¥6.31 (January 2012)
1 yuan (¥) = 100 fen
The yuan is called renminbi (RMB) in China

LAND USE

Arable land 14.86 percent; permanent crops 1.27 percent; protected areas 14.7 percent; other 69.17 percent

UNEMPLOYMENT RATE

4.3 percent (September 2009 est.)
Note: Official data for urban areas only; including migrants may boost total unemployment to 9 percent; there is substantial unemployment and underemployment in rural areas.

AGRICULTURAL PRODUCTS

World leader in gross value of agricultural output; rice, wheat, potatoes, corn, peanuts, tea, millet, barley, apples, cotton, oilseed, pork, fish

MAJOR EXPORTS

Electrical and other machinery; including data-processing equipment; apparel; textiles; iron and steel; optical and medical equipment

MAJOR IMPORTS

Electrical and other machinery, oil and mineral fuels, optical and medical equipment, metal ores, plastics, organic chemicals

MAJOR TRADING PARTNERS

United States, Japan, South Korea, Germany

INTERNET ACCESS

Service providers (ISPs): 6 (2010)
Users: 477 million (2011)

CULTURAL CHINA

Grand Buddha
The 233-foot (71-m) sculpture is the largest Buddha in the world, located at Leshan in Sichuan province. Construction began in A.D. 714, and was completed 90 years later.

Qinghai Lake (Koko Nor)
China's largest fish-rich lake is 10,500 feet (3,200 m) above sea level and 186 miles (300 km) west of Qinghai's capital city, Xining. The main attraction here is Bird Island, a breeding ground for wild geese, gulls, cormorants, sandpipers, and other species.

Forbidden City
The Forbidden City in Beijing, once off-limits to the common people, was home to emperors of the Ming and Qing dynasties. Construction was completed in 1420 after the Ming rulers moved the capital to Beijing. Also called the Palace Museum, the City was looted heavily during the Japanese invasion. The Kuomintang also removed valuable relics and treasures.

Great Wall
Construction of one of the Seven Wonders of the ancient world began in the 7th century B.C. when vassal states started building walls to fend off invading forces. With China unified under Qin rule in 221 B.C., segments of the wall were joined to keep out northern invaders.

Harbin
The capital city of Heilongjiang, the northernmost province of China. The city is famous for its Ice Lantern Festival in winter, with fanciful sculptures of various shapes and forms of animals, people, and plants.

Potala Palace
Located in Lhasa, the Potala Palace was built between 1642 and 1650 for the fifth Dalai Lama. Later it was home to the Tibetan government. It was slightly damaged during Tibetan resistance to the Chinese invasion in 1959.

Jiuzhaigou National Park
A nature reserve in northern Sichuan with peaks, waterfalls, ponds, lakes, and forests. The area also has several Tibetan settlements.

Guilin
Guilin is China's world-famous picture-perfect city of mountains and lakes. The famed city was founded during the Qin Dynasty and developed as a transportation hub. During the 1930s and World War II, Guilin was a stronghold of the communists.

Three Gorges
China's famous Three Gorges straddles two provinces—the Qutang and Wuxia gorges in Sichuan province and the Xiling gorge in Hubei province. Limestone cliffs tower on either side of China's longest river, the Yangtze. The scenic Three Gorges was submerged as a result of the construction of the world's largest dam, the Three Gorges Dam, completed in 2006.

The Bund
Shanghai's lengthy waterfront overlooking the Huangpu River boasts colonial architecture that is reminiscent of the city's past as the greatest commercial city in the East. The bund is an Anglo-Indian term.

ABOUT THE CULTURE

OFFICIAL NAME
People's Republic of China

CAPITAL
Beijing

GOVERNMENT
One-party rule (China Communist Party) that allows some free-market principles

DESCRIPTION OF FLAG
Red background with five yellow stars in the top left corner

NATIONAL ANTHEM
"Yi Yong Jun Jin Xing Qu" ("March of the Volunteers")

POPULATION
1.3 billion (2011 estimate)

LIFE EXPECTANCY
74.68 years (2011 estimate)

ETHNIC GROUPS
Han Chinese 92 percent; minorities 8 percent

OFFICIAL RELIGIONS
Taoism 31 percent; Buddhism 20 percent; traditional tribal religions 10 percent; Christians 4 percent; Muslims 2 percent; atheist 15 percent; nonreligious 18 percent

LITERACY RATE
94 percent (2011 estimate)

OFFICIAL LANGUAGE
Putonghua (Mandarin)

NATIONAL HOLIDAYS
New Year's Day (January 1), Spring Festival (January or February), Labor Day (May 1), National Day (October 1)

LEADERS IN SPORTS
Yao Ming—retired professional basketball player; last played for the Houston Rockets

Hou Yifan—Women's World Chess Champion

Shen Xue and Zhao Hongbo—one of the best pair skating teams of all time and 2010 Olympic champions

Li Na—first woman tennis player from China to win a Grand Slam title

Lin Dan—only badminton player in history to have won three consecutive titles at the World Championships

Liu Xiang—world record holder, world champion, and Olympic champion; won first place in 110-m (361-feet) hurdles races in three successive Asian Games

TIME LINE

IN CHINA	IN THE WORLD

221–206 B.C.
Qin Shi Huang unites China.

A.D. 24
Paper is invented.

1000
The Chinese perfect gunpowder and begin to use it in warfare.

1206–1368
Genghis Khan unifies the Mongols and starts conquest of the world. At its height, the Mongol Empire under Kublai Khan stretches from China to Persia and parts of Europe and Russia.

1776
U.S. Declaration of Independence

1789–99
The French Revolution

1839–64
The Chinese are defeated in the Opium Wars; Hong Kong is ceded to Britain.

1911
Sun Yat-sen establishes the Republic.

1919
May Fourth Movement

1914
World War I begins.

1921
Chinese Communist Party is founded.

1925
Sun Yat-sen dies; Chiang Kai-shek succeeds and heads the Nationalists.

1934–35
The Long March

1937
Outbreak of Sino-Japanese War

1939
World War II begins.

1949
The People's Republic of China is founded; Chiang's forces escape to Taiwan.

1945
The United States drops atomic bombs on Hiroshima and Nagasaki. World War II ends.

1958
The Great Leap Forward

1966–76
The Cultural Revolution

1976
Zhou Enlai and Mao Zedong die.

IN CHINA	IN THE WORLD

1989
Army quashes student demonstrations at Tiananmen Square; Jiang Zemin comes to power.

1997
Deng Xiaoping dies; Hong Kong is returned to China.

1998
Zhu Rongji succeeds Li Peng as premier.

2001
China joins the World Trade Organization.

2001
Terrorists crash planes into New York, Washington D.C., and Pennsylvania.

2003
The National People's Congress elects Hu Jintao as president, replacing Jiang Zemin. Severe acute respiratory syndrome (SARS) epidemic hits China. China launches its first manned spacecraft.

2003
War in Iraq begins.

2004
Eleven Asia countries are hit by giant tsunami, killing at least 225,000 people.

2005
Taiwan's National Party leader, Lien Chan, visits China for the first meeting between Nationalist and Communist Party leaders since 1949.

2005
Hurricane Katrina devastates the Gulf Coast of the United States.

2006
Work on the structure of the Three Gorges Dam is completed.

2008
Violent anti-China protests in Tibet are the worst in 20 years. A massive earthquake hits Sichuan Province; Beijing hosts the Olympic Games. Nearly 53,000 Chinese children fall ill after drinking tainted milk.

2009
China celebrates 60 years of Communist Party rule.

2009
Outbreak of flu virus H1N1 around the world

2010
Vice President Xi Jinping is named vice chairman of the powerful Central Military Commission.

2011
Twin earthquake and tsunami disasters strike northeast Japan, leaving over 14,000 dead and thousands more missing.

GLOSSARY

chi
The energy or life force that flows through all living things

fan (fun)
Rice

feng shui
The art of living in harmony with the physical environment so as to attract good fortune

Guanyin
Chinese goddess of mercy

guanxi (KWAHNG-see)
Interpersonal relationships that benefit the parties involved through the exchange of favors

Han
China's ethnic majority

huaqiao (hu-ah-chi-ow)
Overseas Chinese

laoshi (LA-OW sheh)
A term of respect meaning "teacher"

loess
A loamy deposit formed by wind, usually yellowish

mien (me-an)
Noodles

pinyin
A system of writing Chinese words in the English alphabet

Putonghua
China's official language, also known as Mandarin

qigong
A martial art practiced as a form of therapeutic exercise

taijiquan (tie-chi-chuan)
Chinese shadow boxing

weiqi (way-chee)
Chinese board game played with black and white markers. *Wei* means "to surround," while *qi* means "board game."

wushu
A collective name for different forms of Chinese martial arts, the most popular being Chinese boxing (as seen in kung fu movies) where hands and legs move lightning fast, with long, high jumps.

xian sheng (si-anh shehng)
A term of address meaning "Mr." For example, *Mao Zedong Xian Sheng* means Mr. Mao Zedong.

yang
The active life force or energy. Yang is masculinity, sun, heat, and fire.

yin
The passive life force or energy. Yin is represented by femininity, darkness, cold, and water.

FOR FURTHER INFORMATION

BOOKS

Bratt, Kay. *Silent Tears: A Journey of Hope in a Chinese Orphanage*. Seattle: AmazonEncore, e-book, 2010.

Chang, Leslie T. *Factory Girls: From Village to City in a Changing China*. New York: Spiegel & Grau, 2009.

Chen, Guidi and Wu Chuntao. *Will the Boat Sink the Water? The Life of China's Peasants*. New York: PublicAffairs Books, 2007.

Chow, Gregory C. *China's Economic Transformation*, 2nd ed. Princeton, NJ: Wiley-Blackwell, 2007.

Evans, Karin. *The Lost Daughters of China: Adopted Girls, Their Journey to America, and the Search for a Missing Past*. New York: Tarcher, 2008.

National Geographic. *National Geographic Atlas of China*. Washington, D.C.: National Geographic, 2007.

Pomfret, John. *Chinese Lessons: Five Classmates and the Story of the New China*. New York: Holt Paperbacks, 2007.

WEBSITES

The Central People's Government of the People's Republic of China. www.gov.cn/english/
China Daily USA. http://usa.chinadaily.com.cn/
China.org.cn. www.china.org.cn
China Sports Today. www.chinasportstoday.com/en/
EconomyWatch: The Chinese Economy. www.economywatch.com/world_economy/china/
Healthy Chinese Recipes. www.healthychineserecipes.com/
The International Fund for China's Environment. www.ifce.org/
Ministry of Environmental Protection, the People's Republic of China. http://english.mep.gov.cn/
Population Reference Bureau. www.prb.org (type "China" in the search box)
The World Bank. http://go.worldbank.org/HPIGQ0C3O0

VIDEOS/DVDs

China: A Century of Revolution. Zeitgeist Films, 2007.
China from the Inside. PBS, 2007.
China Rises: A Documentary in Four Parts. Discovery, 2008.
Wild China. BBC Warner, 2008.

MUSIC

Chen Wenjie. *The Very Best of Chinese Music*. Arc Music, 2005.
Various Artists. *Eleven Centuries of Traditional Chinese Music*. Legacy International, 2009.
Various Artists. *Heavenly Bamboo and Silk Strings*. Jks Records, 2007.

BIBLIOGRAPHY

BOOKS

Bergsten, Fred C., Charles Freeman, Nicholas R. Lardy, and Derek J. Mitchell. *China's Rise: Challenges and Opportunities.* Washington, DC: Peterson Institute for International Economics, 2009.

Giles, Herbert Allen. *The Civilization of China* (Elibron Classics series edition). Publishing in Motion, 2011.

Jacques, Martin. *When China Rules the World: The End of the Western World and the Birth of a New Global Order.* New York: Penguin Press HC, 2009.

Kynge, James. *China Shakes the World: A Titan's Rise and Troubled Future—and the Challenge for America.* Boston: Mariner Books, 2007.

Lampton, David M. *The Three Faces of Chinese Power: Might, Money, and Minds.* Berkeley, CA: University of California Press, 2008.

Sutter, Robert G. *Chinese Foreign Relations: Power and Policy Since the Cold War* (Asia in World Politics). Lanham, MD: Rowman & Littlefield Publishers, 2009.

WEBSITES

BBC News: How China Is Ruled. www.bbc.co.uk/news/world-asia-pacific-13908155

China for Kids. http://china.mrdonn.org/dynasties.html

China Hush: Family Portraits of All 56 Ethnic Groups in China. www.chinahush.com/2009/12/06/family-portraits-of-all-56-ethnic-groups-in-china/

ChinaToday.com: China Economy. www.chinatoday.com/china.topics/china_economy.htm

Chinese Childbook.com: Chinese Games for Kids. www.childbook.com/Chinese-Children-Game-Instructions-s/79.htm

Chinese Fortune Calendar: Where Does the Yin-Yang Symbol Come From? www.chinesefortunecalendar.com/yinyang.htm

Chinese Knot Weddings: Chinese Wedding Games. www.chineseknotweddings.com/traditional/chinese-wedding-games

Chinese Language. www.chineselanguage.com

Chinese New Year: Chinese Paper Cutting for Kids. www.chinesenewyear.me/chinese-paper-cutting-for-kids.html

CIA—the World Factbook: China. https://www.cia.gov/library/publications/the-world-factbook/geos/ch.html

First Palette: Chinese Opera Mask. www.firstpalette.com/Craft_themes/World/Chinese_Opera_Mask/Chinese_Opera_Mask.html

The Green Reason. http://thegreenreason.com/

International Fund for China's Environment: Wildlife in China. www.ifce.org/pages/conservation.html

Kidipede: History for Kids. www.historyforkids.org/learn/china/history/index.htm

KidsPast.com: Civilization in China. www.kidspast.com/world-history/0125-civilization-in-china.php

National Geographic Kids: China Facts and Pictures. http://kids.nationalgeographic.com/kids/places/find/china/

The Nature Conservancy: China. www.nature.org/ourinitiatives/regions/asiaandthepacific/china/

Top China Travel. www.topchinatravel.com

INDEX

INDEX